Animalia

from the
Royal
Collection

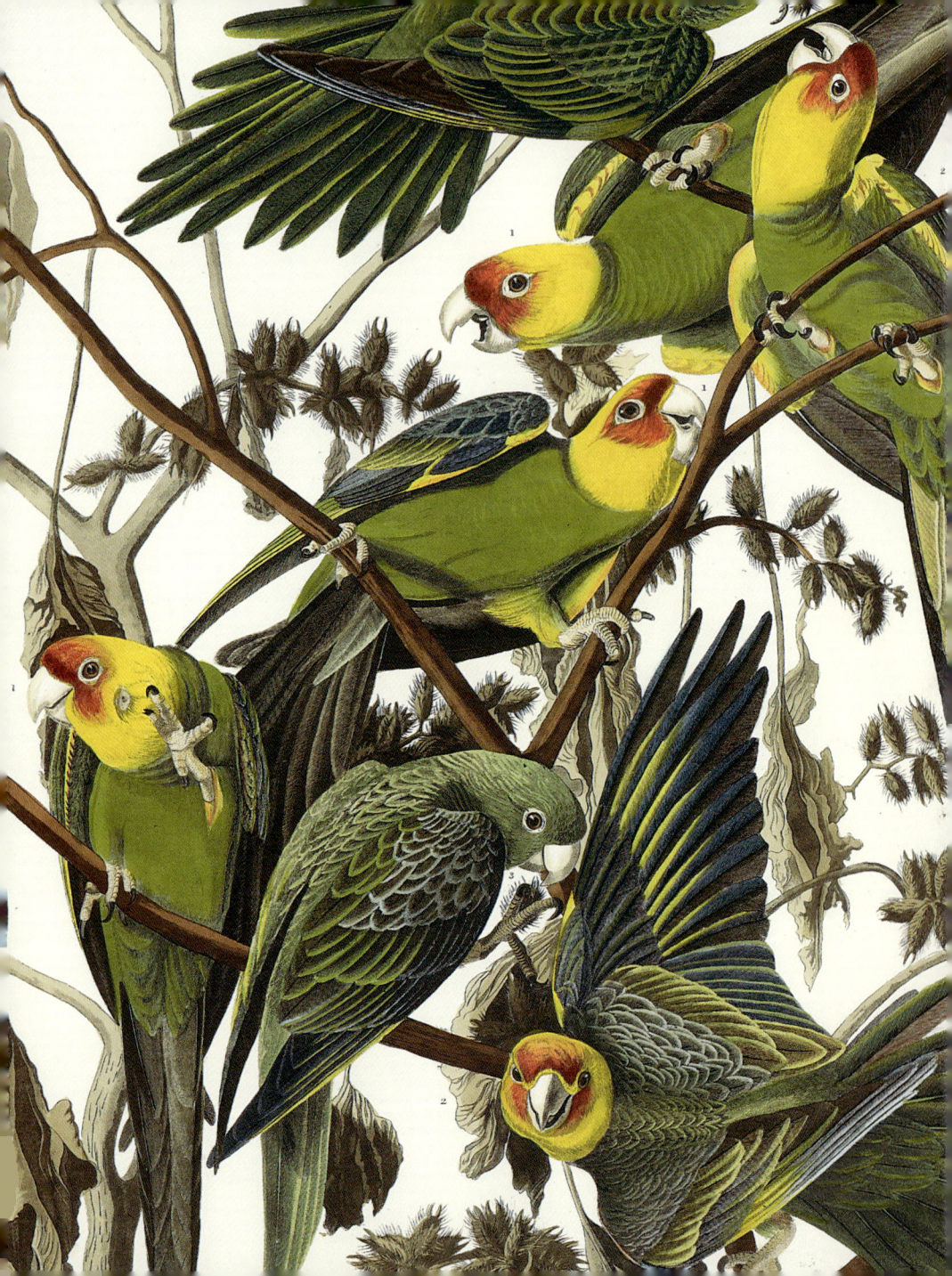

Animalia

from the
Royal
Collection

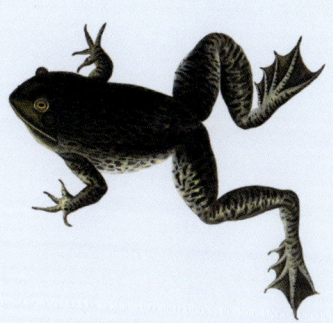

ROYAL COLLECTION TRUST

Animalia from the Royal Collection

The natural world has been of great interest to royalty for centuries, from the menageries of medieval kings to the kitchen and physic gardens of the Tudor and Stuart monarchs, the aviaries and botanical gardens of the Georgians and Victorians through to His Majesty King Charles III's own initiatives to support biodiversity, sustainability and the environment today. As a result, the Royal Collection is brimming with beautiful examples of natural history art assembled by generations of royal collectors.

The items chosen for this book, from the collections of the Royal Library and Print Room at Windsor Castle, date to the eighteenth and nineteenth centuries, the 'golden age' of European natural history illustration. As Britain and other nations expanded their influence overseas, specimens of new and exotic plants and animals began to be brought back by merchants and explorers. These were regularly placed in scientific institutions or cabinets of curiosities, the forerunners of the modern museum. Such collections inspired generations of naturalists, who ventured abroad or looked closely at the animals found closer to home. Their discoveries brought into question long-standing beliefs about humanity's place in the world.

In 1699, Maria Sibylla Merian, inspired by the wonders arriving in Amsterdam where she was then living, embarked on a voyage to Suriname in South America, then a Dutch colony. Travelling through the dense rainforest and combatting the harsh environment, Merian was able to observe and draw the entire life cycles of insects. On her return to the Netherlands in 1701, she began preparing her drawings for publication as *Metamorphosis Insectorum Surinamensium*, dedicated to 'all lovers and investigators of nature'. A group of Merian's illustrations were purchased by George III in 1755 and a deluxe copy of her book was bought by William IV in 1835. Merian's work was innovative in its depiction of insects crawling on or flying around the plants upon which they relied. One can only imagine the excitement of seeing – for the very first time – the huntsman spider or the giant silk moth rendered in such realistic detail.

In Britain, there was a similar passion to encounter hitherto unknown creatures. Spearheaded by collectors such as Sir Hans Sloane, who himself had travelled to Jamaica in 1687 and had learned about the island's biodiversity from colonists and people enslaved on its plantations, expeditions were undertaken to North America to reveal the marvels of the continent. In 1722, Sloane was a chief supporter of a voyage to the Carolinas and Florida by the English naturalist and skilled artist Mark Catesby. This was Catesby's second visit to America, driven by a 'passionate desire' to witness the beauty of nature and the urge to draw specimens from life. He travelled along the Savannah River into regions little known to Europeans and made minute studies of birds, fish, mammals and amphibians. On his return to London, he set about publishing his findings in his *Natural History of Carolina, Florida and the Bahama Islands*. Demand was so great that Catesby struggled to meet deadlines, taking 16 years to complete the publication. Purchased by George III in 1768, Catesby's books and drawings are among the finest treasures of the Royal Collection.

Despite their passion for nature, it is impossible to disassociate Merian and Catesby from wider issues. Both naturalists received patronage from individuals who had made substantial profits from the enslavement of others. Both also made use of enslaved or Indigenous people who were sent ahead to clear a path through dense foliage, carried heavy luggage or helped identify specimens. Such 'retainers' formed a significant part of many European natural history expeditions in the eighteenth and nineteenth centuries.

* * *

Louis Renard's *Poissons, Ecrevisses et Crabes* (1718–19, second edition 1754), a collection of illustrations of tropical fish all reportedly found in the seas off Indonesia, offers a contrast to the work of naturalists such as Merian and Catesby who ventured overseas to draw animals from life. The artists employed by Renard to illustrate the book depicted fish and crustaceans in an eclectic range of eye-catching, psychedelic colours that bore little relation to those of the living creatures. Although Renard declared his work accurate, the colouring of the fish, his recommendations of sauces to serve with them, and the inclusion of fantastical creatures undermined his claims. However, many species depicted in his book have since been identified as living in those waters.

Fish

From Louis Renard,
*Poissons, Ecrevisses
et Crabes*, 1718–19

RCIN 1057041

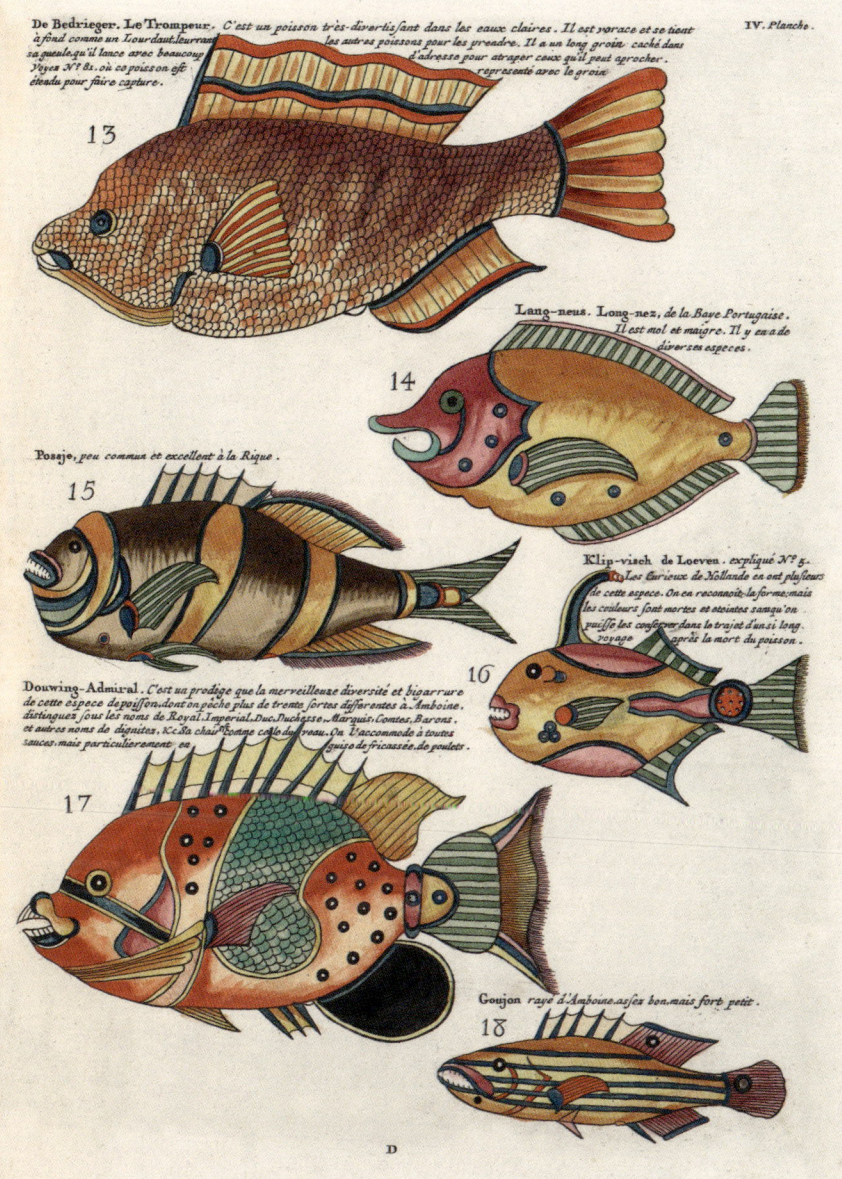

De Bedrieger. Le Trompeur. C'est un poisson très-divertissant dans les eaux claires. Il est vorace et se tient à fond comme un Lourdaut leurrant les autres poissons pour les prendre. Il a un long groin caché dans sa gueule qu'il lance avec beaucoup d'adresse pour atraper ceux qu'il peut aprocher. Voyez N.° 81. où ce poisson est représenté avec le groin étendu pour faire capture.

IV. Planche.

13

Lang-neus. Long-nez, de la Baye Portugaise. Il est mol et maigre. Il y en a de diverses especes.

14

Possje, peu commun et excellent à la Rique.

15

Klip-visch de Loeven. expliqué N.° 5. Les Curieux de Hollande en ont plusieurs de cette espece. On en reconnoit la forme, mais les couleurs sont mortes et eteintes tansqu'on puisse les conserver dans le trajet d'un si long voyage après la mort du poisson.

16

Douwing-Admiral. C'est un prodige que la merveilleuse diversité et bigarrure de cette espece de poisson, dont on pèche plus de trente sortes differentes à Amboine, distinguez sous les noms de Royal. Imperial. Duc. Duchesse. Marquis. Comtes. Barons. et autres noms de dignités. Ke. Sa chair comme celle du veau. On l'accommode à toutes sauces, mais particulierement en guise de fricassée de poulets.

17

Goujon rayé d'Amboine, assez bon, mais fort petit.

18

D

In the 1780s and 1790s, a little-known London naturalist, Thomas Martyn, established an 'academy' to teach poor boys how to make fine illustrations. Sadly, nothing is known of his pupils beyond the beautiful art they produced. In 1784, Martyn published his *Universal Conchologist*, an attempt to classify and illustrate shells collected in the Pacific during James Cook's three voyages (1768–80). The paintings are stunningly realistic, with even the smallest details reproduced in the most delicate and naturalistic manner. Martyn presented the Prince of Wales, later George IV, with a special copy of his book. He followed the gift with a portfolio of paintings of birds and insects that showcased the skills of his students – including a scarab beetle one can almost touch. The Prince must have been taken with the images and soon acquired Martyn's other books for his library.

Like her predecessor Merian, Sarah Bowdich's *Fresh Water Fishes of Great Britain* (1828) offers an insight into the often-overlooked work of women naturalists in the eighteenth and nineteenth centuries. She demonstrated her talent in observing the natural world while travelling with her husband Thomas Bowdich to the Asante Empire (modern Ghana) where she became the first European woman to collect plants in tropical West Africa. She was encouraged by her friends to publish a book on British freshwater fish and travelled the country catching fish and painting watercolours of them 'immediately [after they] came from the water' to preserve the iridescence of their fins and scales. For fish she could not find, Bowdich enlisted friends to send her living specimens, providing intricate instructions to ensure that they arrived unharmed. She produced more than 1,200 paintings for the fish found in the limited edition of 50 books. Instead of printed illustrations, each book contained original watercolours, all created with an ingenious combination of layers of pigment and gold or silver leaf. The stunning visual effect can be appreciated in her watercolour of a perch, in her opinion 'the finest of our British fishes', which glistens as if ready to swim from the page.

* * *

One of the greatest natural history books in the Royal Collection is John James Audubon's *Birds of America* (1827–38). The four-volume set is of a size known as double elephant folio (approximately 100 × 67 cm). It contains 435 plates of birds, all shown life-size and all depicted as if feeding, hunting, preening, perched, or in flight. To ensure that smaller species would not feel lost on the large pages, he often showed them among foliage, as seen in the vibrant illustration of the now-extinct Carolina parakeet. Other species, including the roseate spoonbill and the great white pelican, were depicted within scenes reminiscent of their habitats, while the largest birds, notably the flamingo, were contorted into unnatural positions to fit on the page. Audubon's work revolutionised ornithological art. Showing each bird as if alive enabled naturalists to appreciate intricate anatomical details, and for those not interested in such matters, the dramatic images were breathtaking.

Audubon based his illustrations on specimens he had observed and hunted while travelling along the westernmost fringes of the United States in the first decades of the nineteenth century. A natural showman, he travelled to Britain in 1826 to gain supporters – among them George IV – and regaled delighted audiences with his tales of the American 'frontier'. Some of his stories were later published in his *Ornithological Biography* (1831–9), a collection of bird biographies and anecdotes which supplemented the magnificent illustrations. While his images are still awe-inspiring, recent research has explored controversial aspects of Audubon's life, particularly his views towards the abolition movement and his treatment of enslaved people.

* * *

In 1832, John Gould published the first volume of his famous 'bird books', which would become perhaps the greatest achievement of ornithological art in Britain. *A Century of Birds from the Himalaya Mountains* depicted a selection of South Asian birds received by Gould in his role as curator of the museum of the Zoological Society of London. Working with his wife, Elizabeth, and the artist Edward Lear, he made drawings and turned them into printed illustrations using the new technology of lithography. Lear taught the Goulds the technique, which allowed for subtle hand-colouring and the reproduction of fine details from the original drawings. Most plates were drawn by Elizabeth, who rendered complex plumage with great accuracy, notable in her magnificent depiction of the technicolour feathers of the Himalayan monal, the national bird of Nepal. The publication, which was dedicated to William IV, was an instant success due to its splendid depiction of birds never seen before in Britain.

The Goulds, in collaboration with Lear and the illustrator Henry Constantine Richter, immediately started work on *The Birds of Europe* (1832–7), which made the Goulds a household name. Elizabeth again provided the bulk of illustrations and Lear, despite his poor eyesight, produced some of the most characterful. John Gould parted with Lear in the years after his return from Australia

Princess of Wales parakeet

From John Gould,
The Birds of Australia,
1869

RCIN 1122380

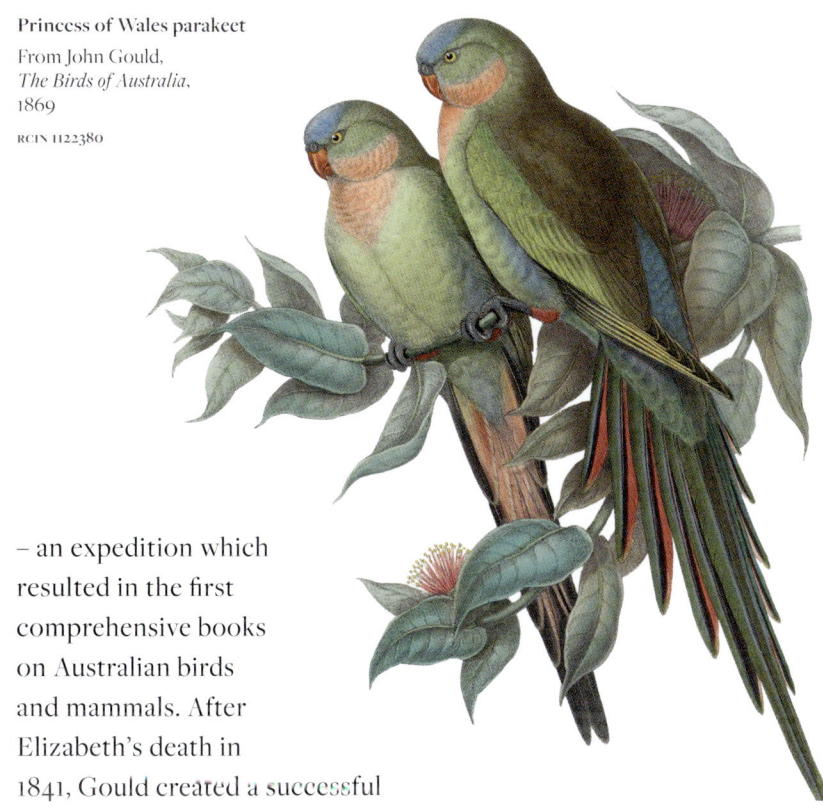

– an expedition which
resulted in the first
comprehensive books
on Australian birds
and mammals. After
Elizabeth's death in
1841, Gould created a successful
workshop of artists that produced multiple books at a time
to meet the demands of his wealthy patrons, among whom, he
boasted, were 'almost all the crowned heads of Europe'.

Gould would make a quick annotated sketch of birds, for his
artists to work up into a more accurate representation. He often
included notes on the types of plants he wanted each bird to
be drawn with and its position on the page, creating the most
picturesque scene for his clients. This process reached its apex
in *The Birds of Great Britain* (1873), which featured images of

all common and rare British birds illustrated to suit Victorian sensibilities: from the domestic vision of a family of long-tailed tits perching on a branch, to the vibrant flash of yellow as a pair of goldfinches squabble over a teasel. However, when preparing the books, Gould encountered difficulties with one of his artists, Joseph Wolf. Described by Sir Edward Landseer as 'the finest animal painter that ever lived', he disliked Gould's strict control over the design of the plates. Wolf was able to capture animals with remarkable realism: red kites ruffle their feathers while falcons meet the viewer's eyes with their piercing gaze.

While Gould viewed *Birds of Great Britain* as the favourite of his publications, it was his hummingbirds that showcased the full potential of lithography and the exceptional detail artists could apply to their illustrations. In 1851, Queen Victoria visited Gould's display of his hummingbird collection at the Zoological Gardens in London. She remarked in her Journal on seeing the delicate birds in specially designed cases that highlighted their jewel-like feathers: 'It is the most beautiful & complete collection ever seen, & it is impossible to imagine anything so lovely as these little Humming Birds, their variety, & the extraordinary brilliancy of their colours.' When the book was published in 1869, the lithographs were enhanced by the innovative use of oil paints and varnish over gold leaf so that the tiny birds twinkled in the gaslight as the pages were turned. Victoria received a complete set which remains in the Royal Collection today.

* * *

As the nineteenth century progressed, the natural sciences became increasingly professionalised and hand-coloured illustrated publications were largely replaced by books printed with photographs. Nevertheless, drawings remained important for identification, as artists were able to capture colours and other details that the camera may have missed. Examples include Frederic Moore's study of Indian butterflies and moths, *Lepidoptera Indica* (1890–1913), and Sir Walter Buller's *Birds of New Zealand* (1873), the first comprehensive survey of that nation's birds. Both were illustrated with hand-finished lithographs that revealed minute variations between species and added a touch of luxury for prospective subscribers. In addition to showcasing iconic New Zealand birds, such as the kākāpō and kiwi, Buller was among the first naturalists to remark on the devastating effects on the islands' biodiversity following the arrival of humans and the introduction of invasive species. He commented on the need to look after these unique animals for future generations.

The natural history illustrations in the Royal Collection offer a glimpse at the world's wondrous biodiversity and serve as reminders of our duty to cherish nature in all its forms. Several species illustrated in this book, including the kākāpō and Carolina parakeet, are vulnerable, endangered or extinct through hunting, habitat loss or climate change. Many others are seeing large declines in their populations. Through the passionate advocacy of Prince Philip, Duke of Edinburgh, and His Majesty The King, the Royal Library has seen its natural history collections focus increasingly on sustainability and the environment, through the acquisition of books that raise awareness of the work that needs to be done by combining new research with beautiful artworks that emulate the 'golden age' of natural history.

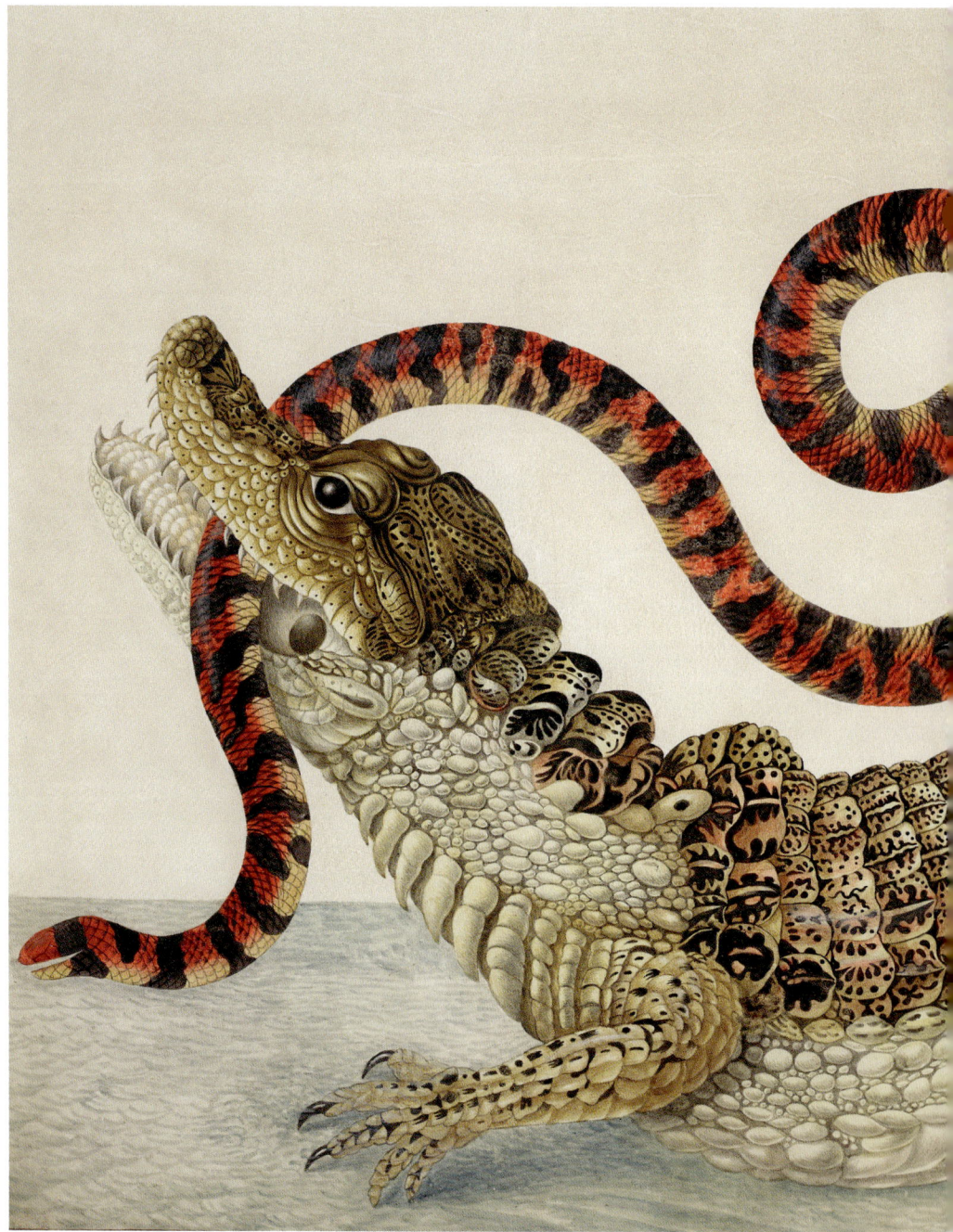

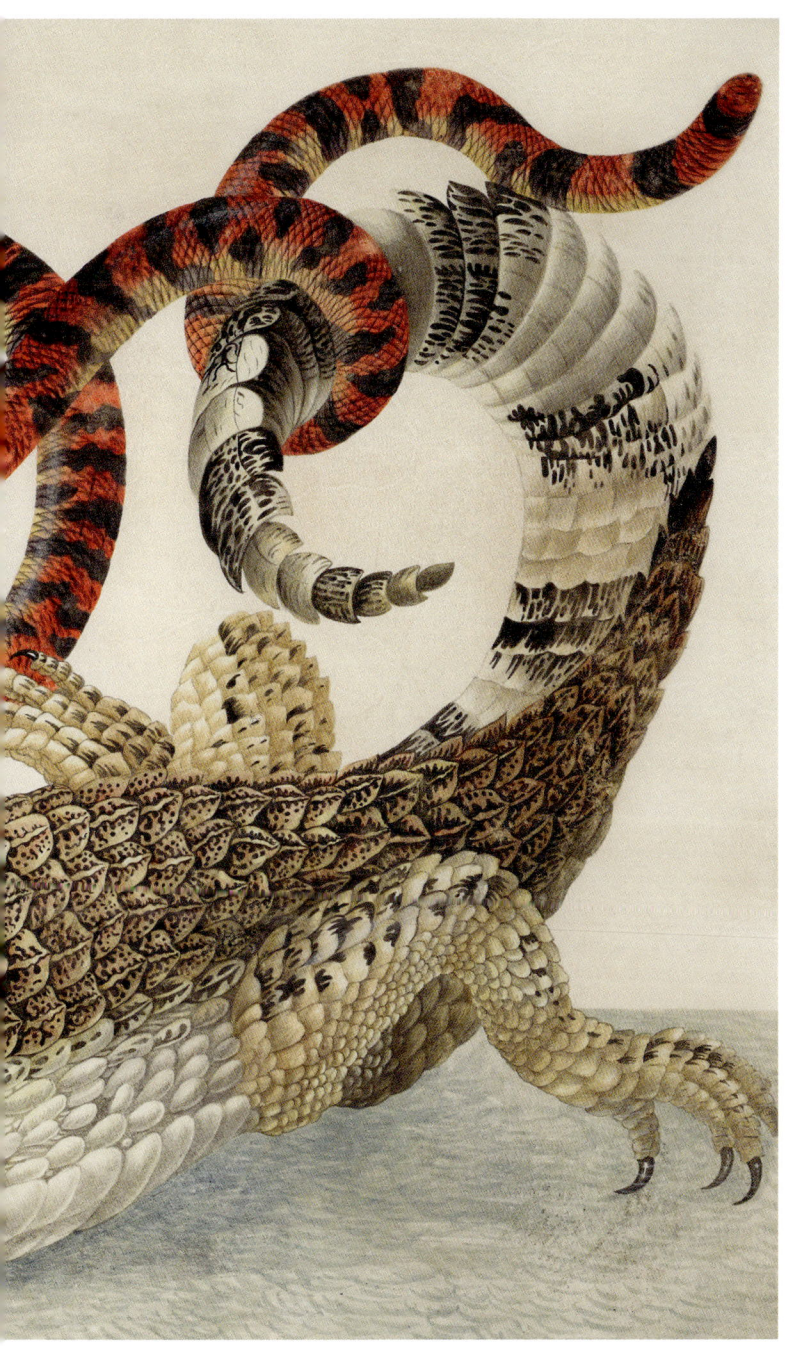

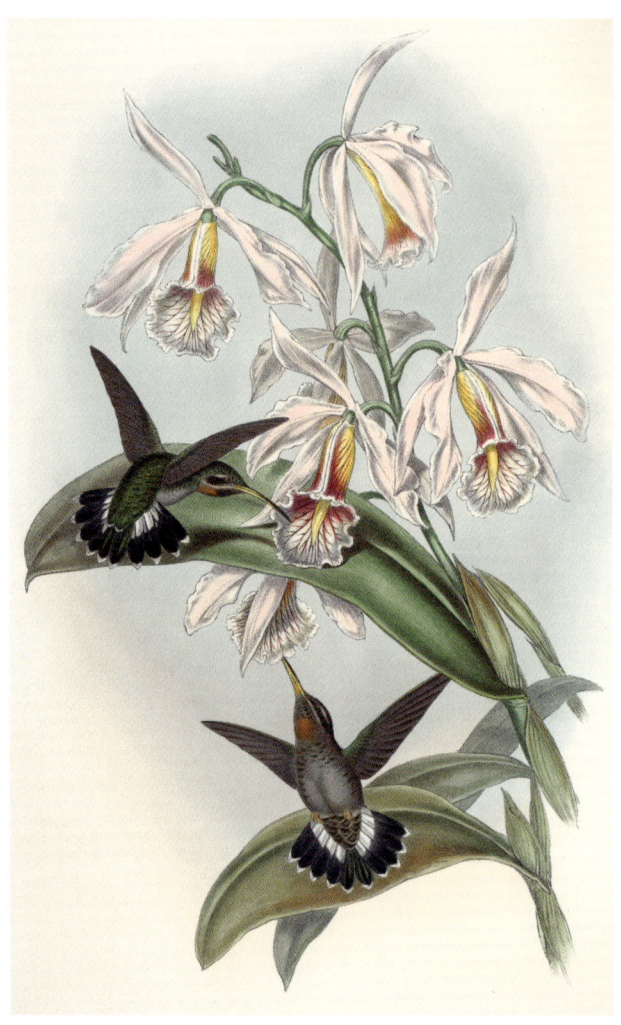

Fraser's hermit

From John Gould,
*A Monograph of the
Trochilidae, or family
of Humming-Birds,*
1861

RCIN 1055254

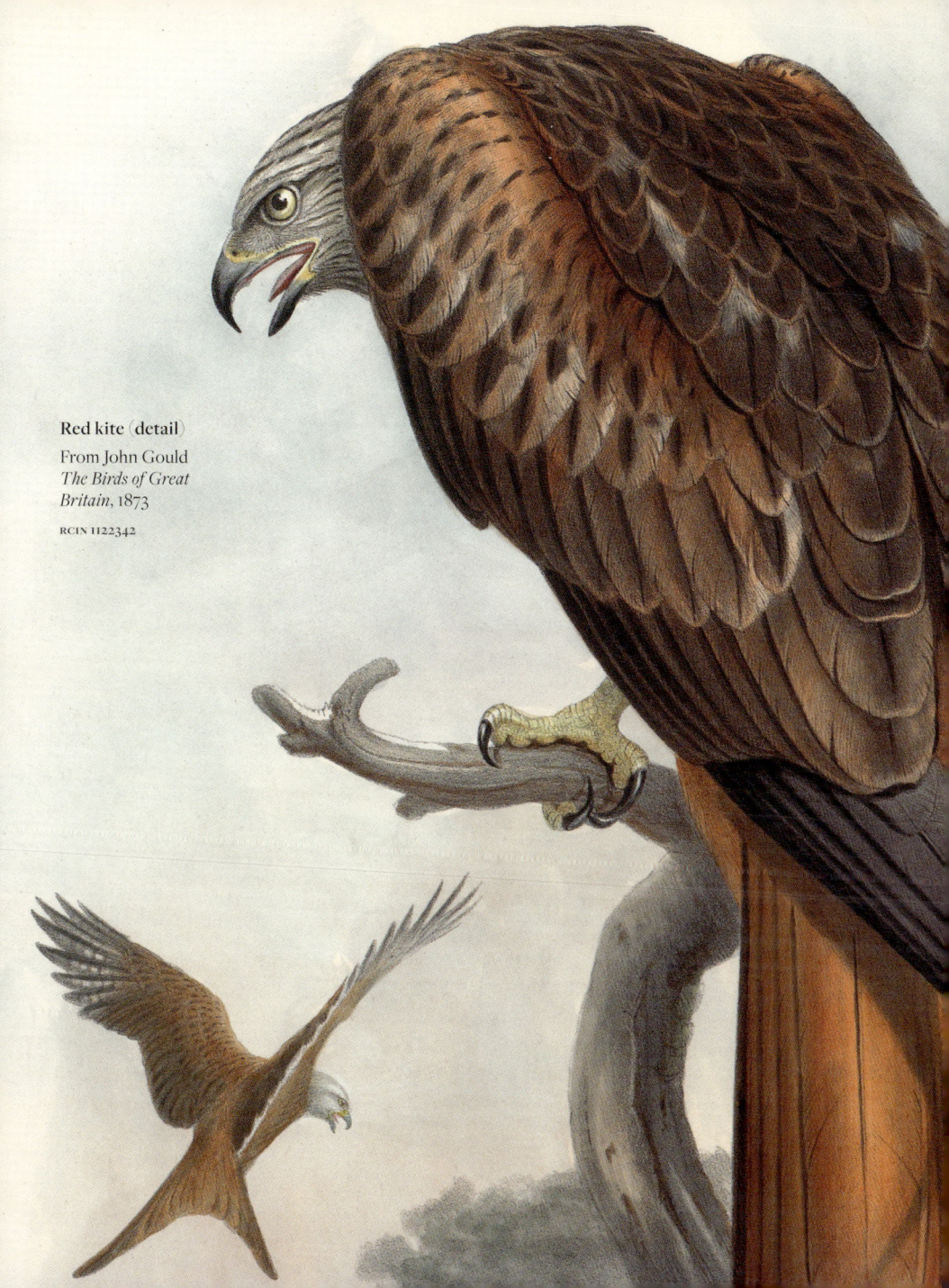

Red kite (detail)

From John Gould
*The Birds of Great
Britain*, 1873

RCIN 1122342

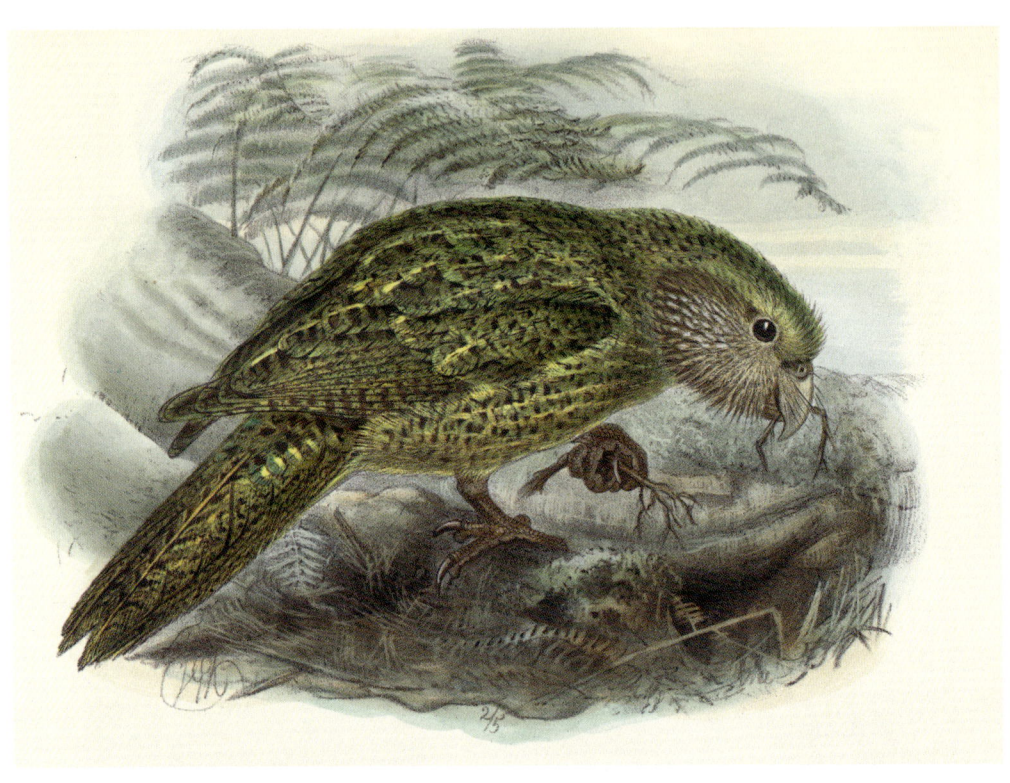

Owl parrot (kākāpō)

From Sir Walter Buller,
*A History of the Birds of
New Zealand*, 1873

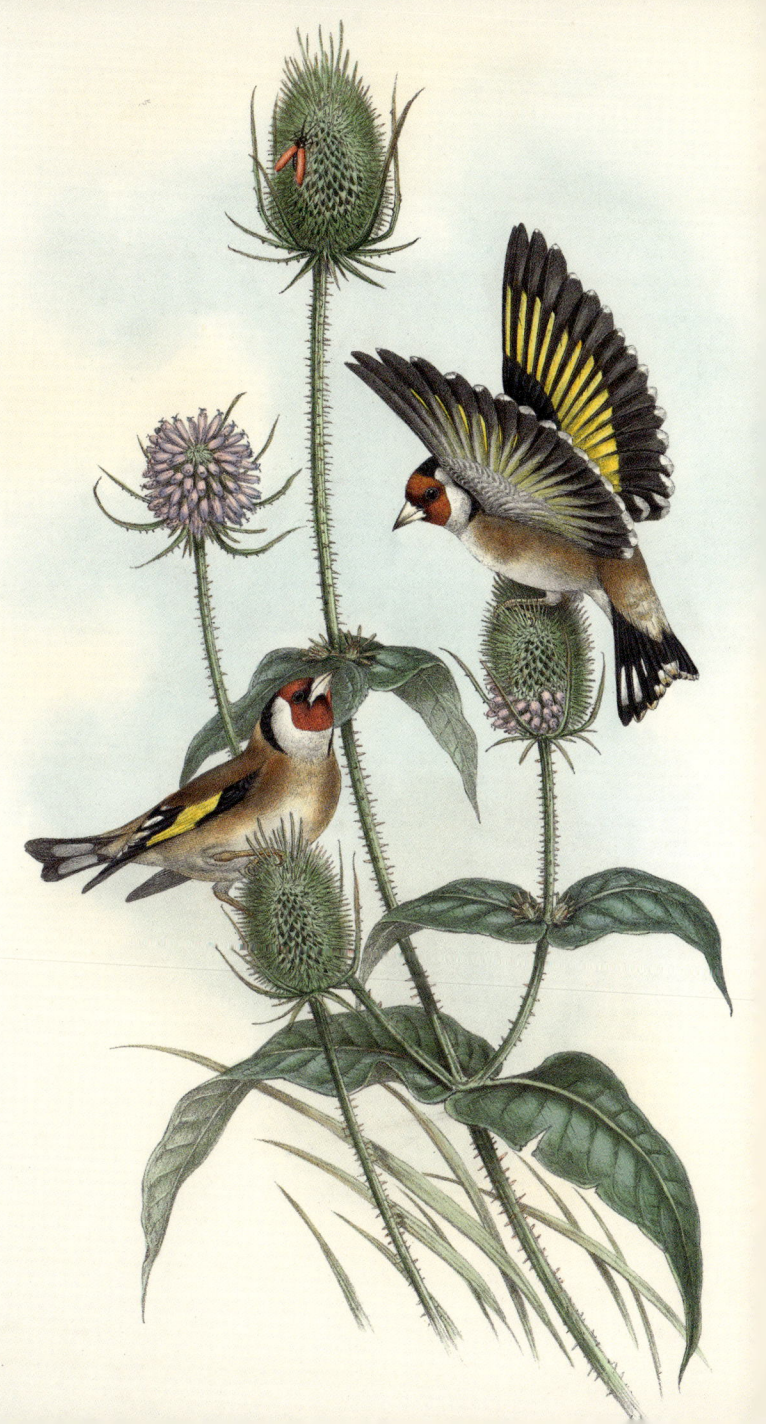

European goldfinch

From John Gould,
*The Birds of Great
Britain*, 1873

RCIN 1122344

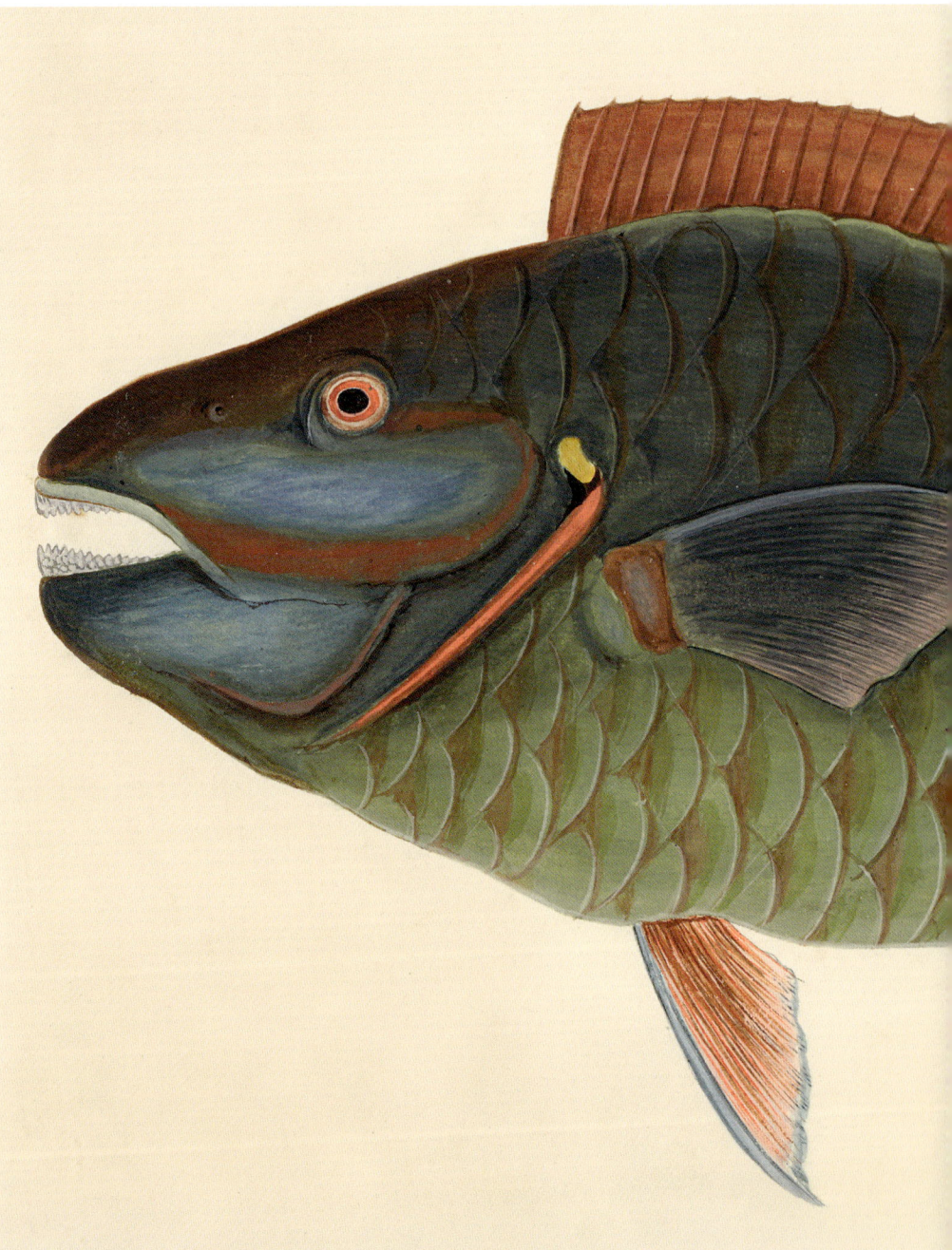

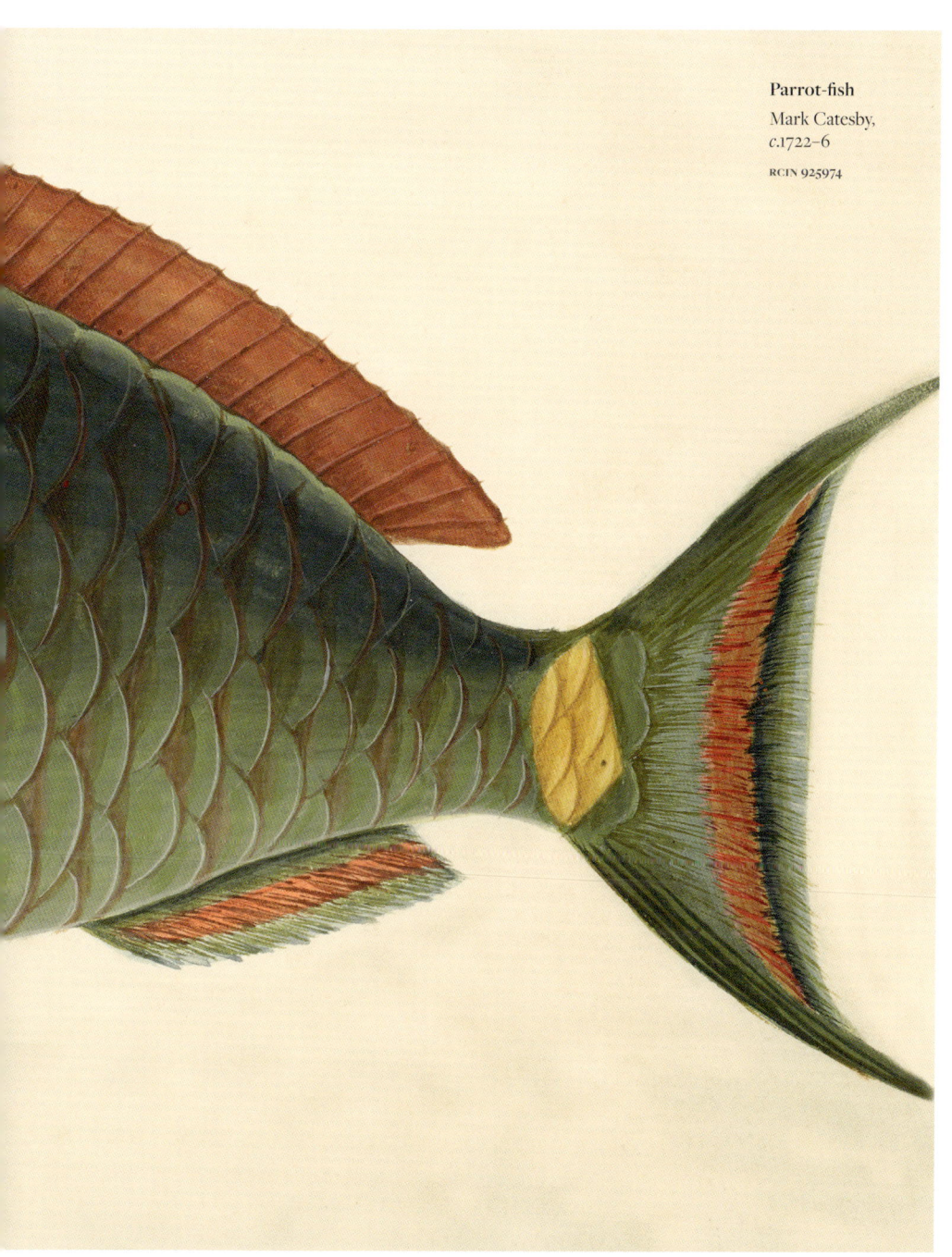

Parrot-fish
Mark Catesby,
*c.*1722–6

RCIN 925974

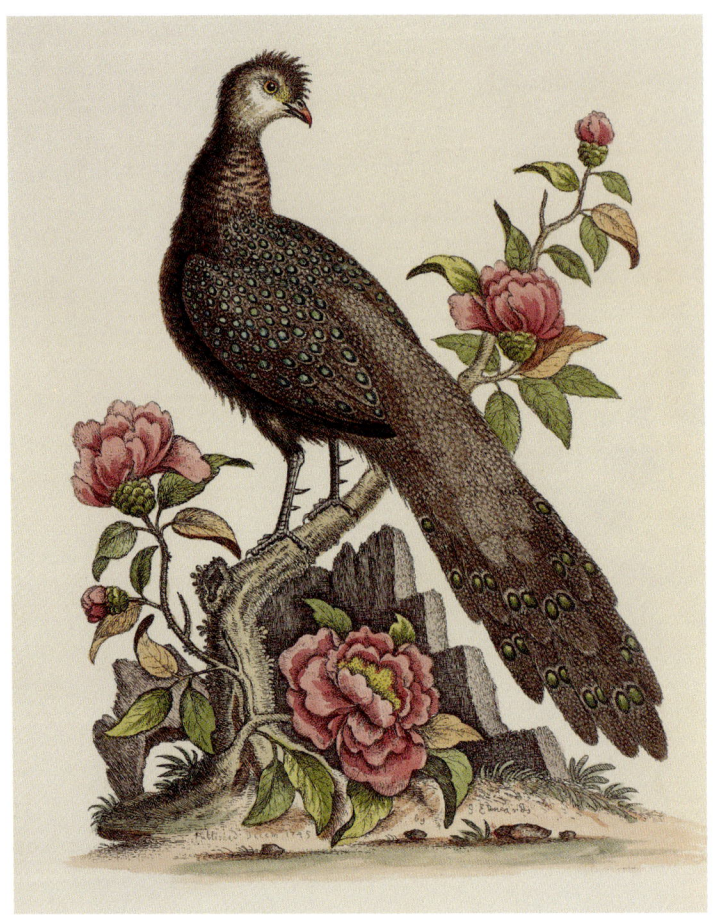

Peacock pheasant from China

From George Edwards,
*A Natural History of
Uncommon Birds*, 1743–7

RCIN 1057008

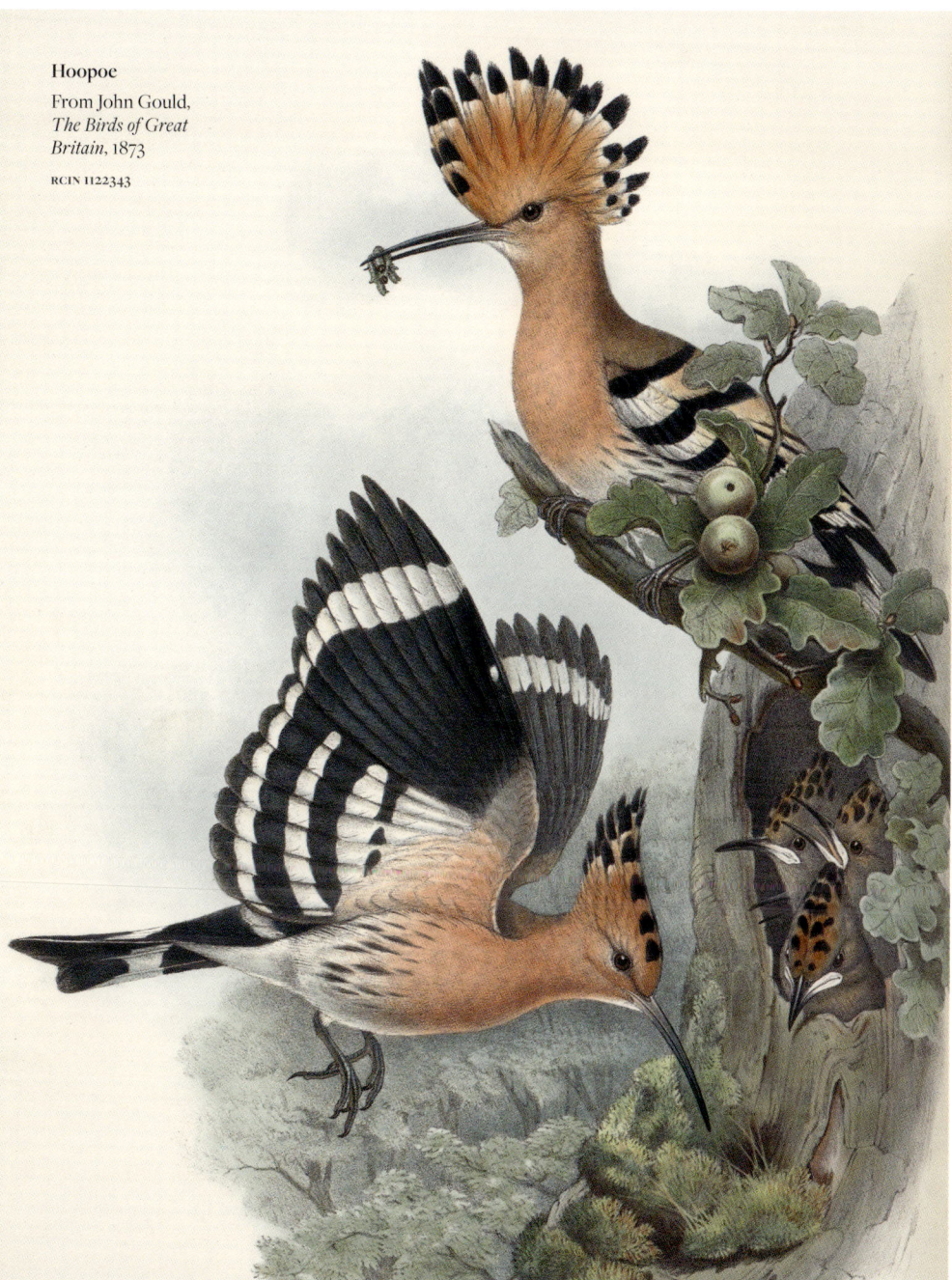

Hoopoe

From John Gould,
*The Birds of Great
Britain*, 1873

RCIN 1122343

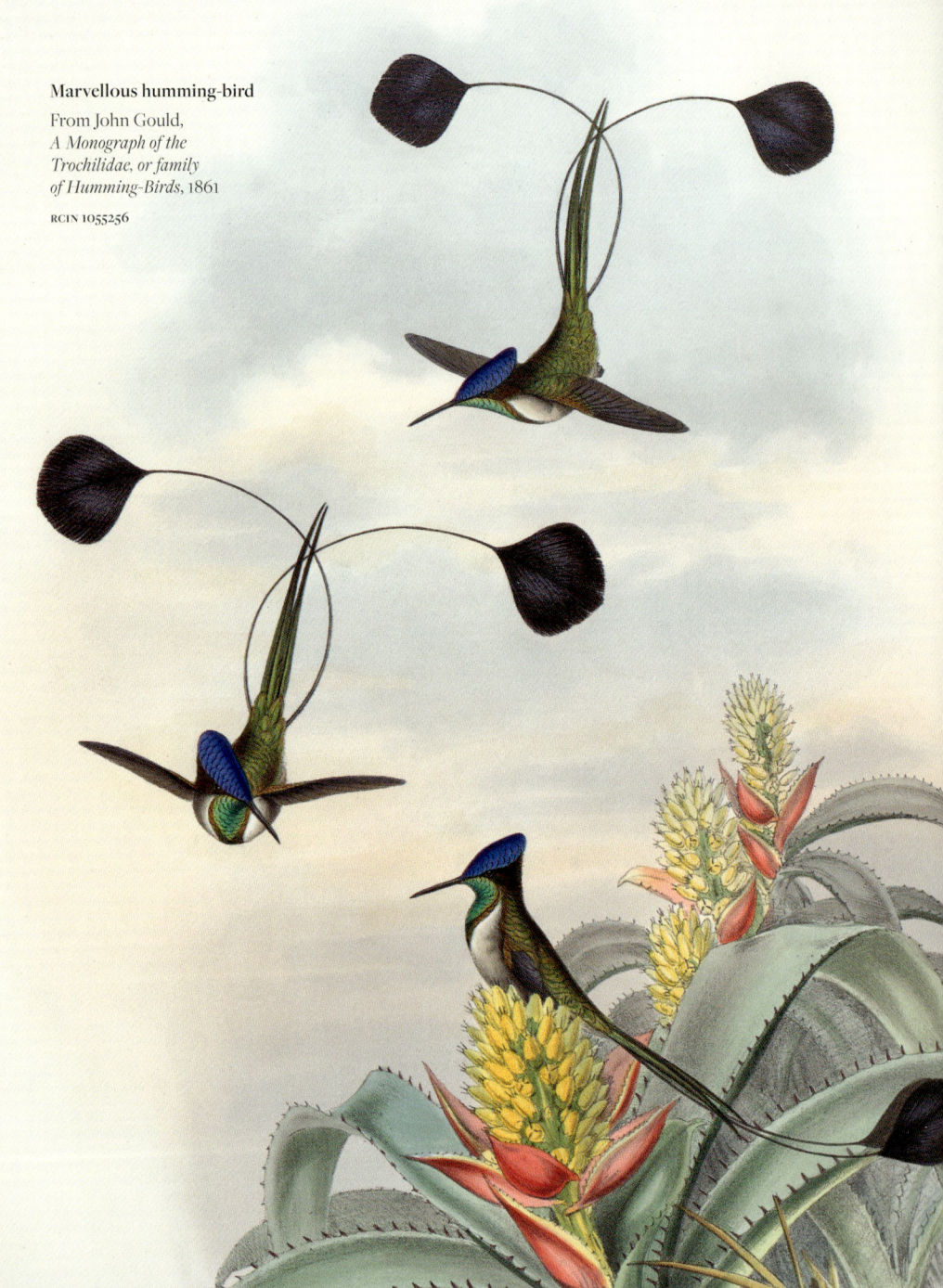

Marvellous humming-bird

From John Gould,
*A Monograph of the
Trochilidae, or family
of Humming-Birds*, 1861

RCIN 1055256

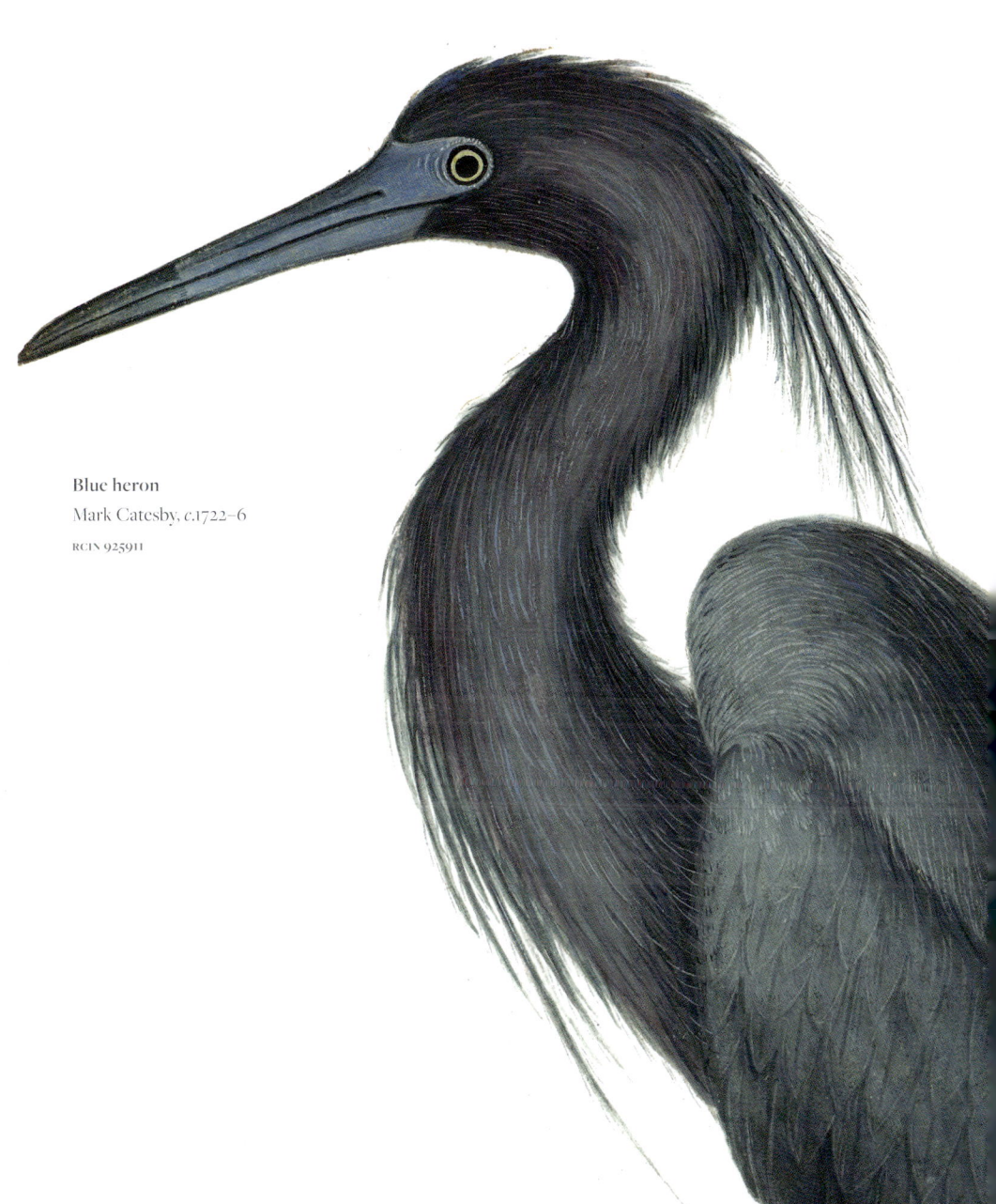

Blue heron
Mark Catesby, c.1722–6
RCIN 925911

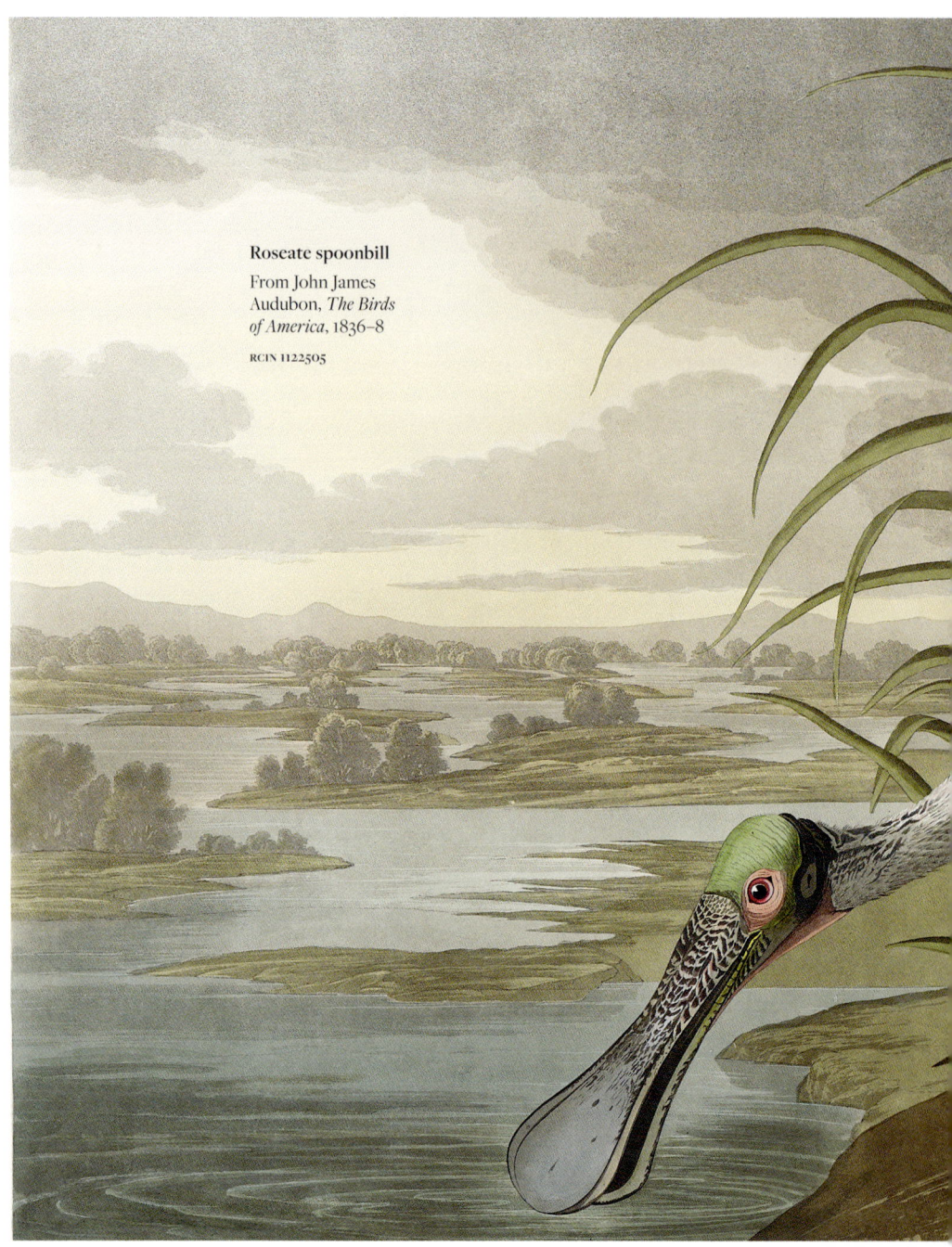

Roseate spoonbill

From John James
Audubon, *The Birds
of America*, 1836–8

RCIN 1122505

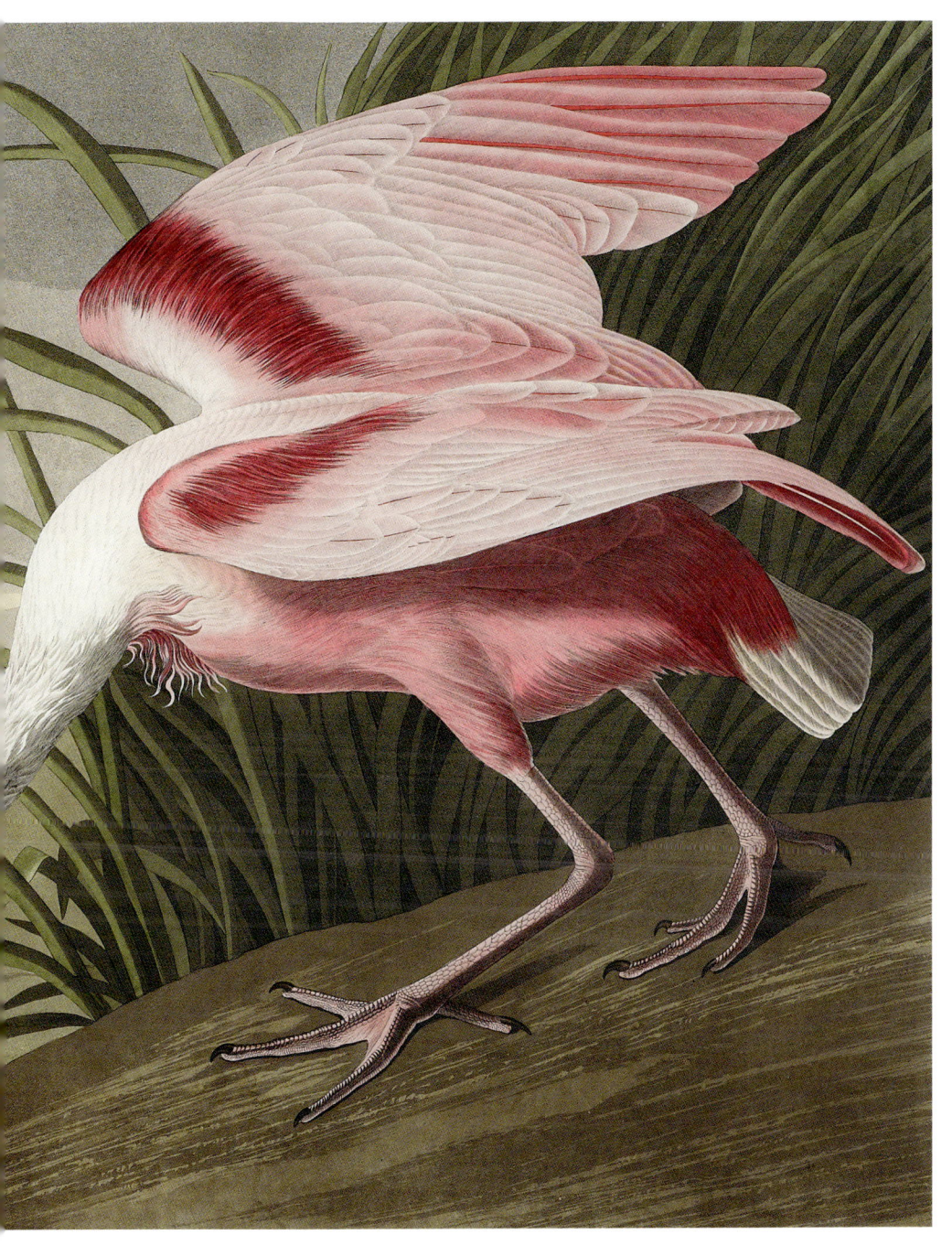

OPPOSITE

Fish and crustaceans

From Louis Renard,
Poissons, Ecrevisses et Crabes, 1754

RCIN 1057042

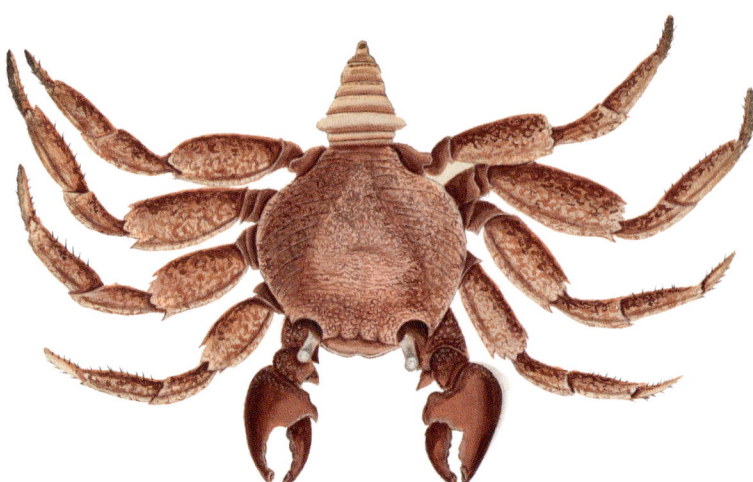

The red mottled
rock-crab and the
rough-shell'd crab

Mark Catesby,
*c.*1722–6

RCIN 925982

Hercules

From Thomas Martyn,
*The Universal
Conchologist*, 1784

RCIN 1122340

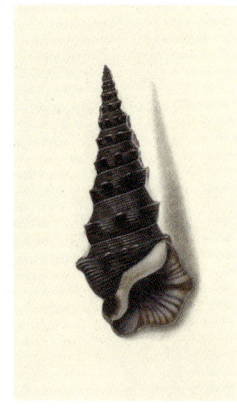
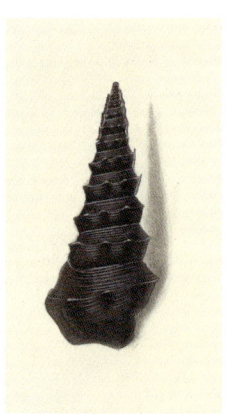

203. Katjang-Roeper. Crabbe-criarde. Elle crie comme un petit chat. et assez haut.

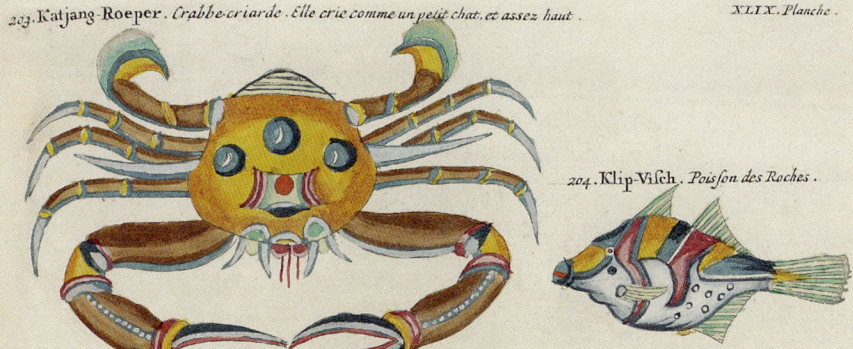

204. Klip-Visch. Poisson des Roches.

205. Kamp-haan d'Amboine. Il est aussi bon et aussi commun que le Goujon qu'on apelle Post en Hollande.

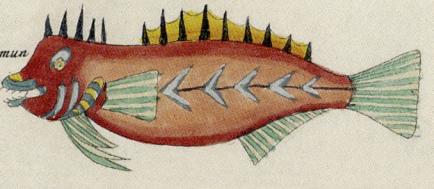

206. Kruys-Krabbe. La Crabbe Sainte de l'Isle de Boutton. Elle est en grande Veneration parmi les Pretres et Missionaires. Les Peres Jesuites disent que St. François Xavier prechant l'Evangile aux Indiens, un Raya, ou Roy en colere luy arracha des mains la Croix qu'il montroit et annonçoit aux peuples, et qu'ayant jetté cette Croix dans la Mer, une Crabbe marquée d'une Croix, comme celle-cy, la raporta dans ses puis sur le Rivage à la vue du Raya et d'une grande foule de peuple qui par ce Miracle furent Convertis a la Foy Chretienne.

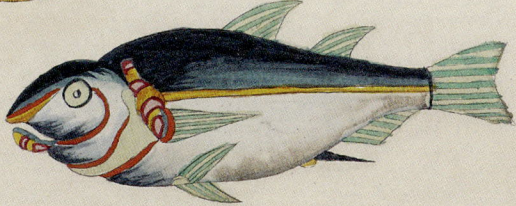

207. Loupert de Baguewall fort bon a la Sauce à l'oseille.

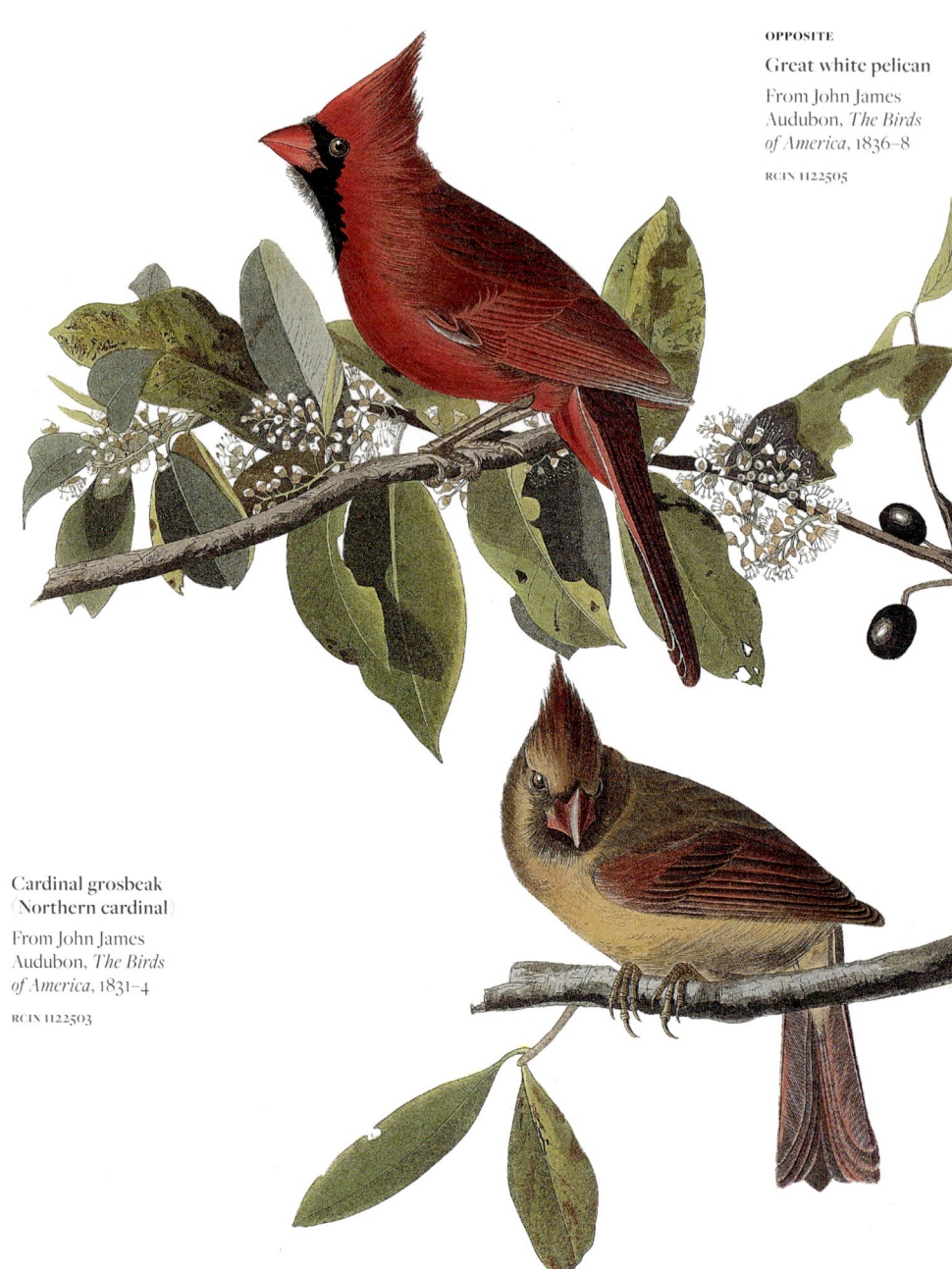

OPPOSITE

Great white pelican

From John James
Audubon, *The Birds
of America*, 1836–8

RCIN 1122505

Cardinal grosbeak
(Northern cardinal)

From John James
Audubon, *The Birds
of America*, 1831–4

RCIN 1122503

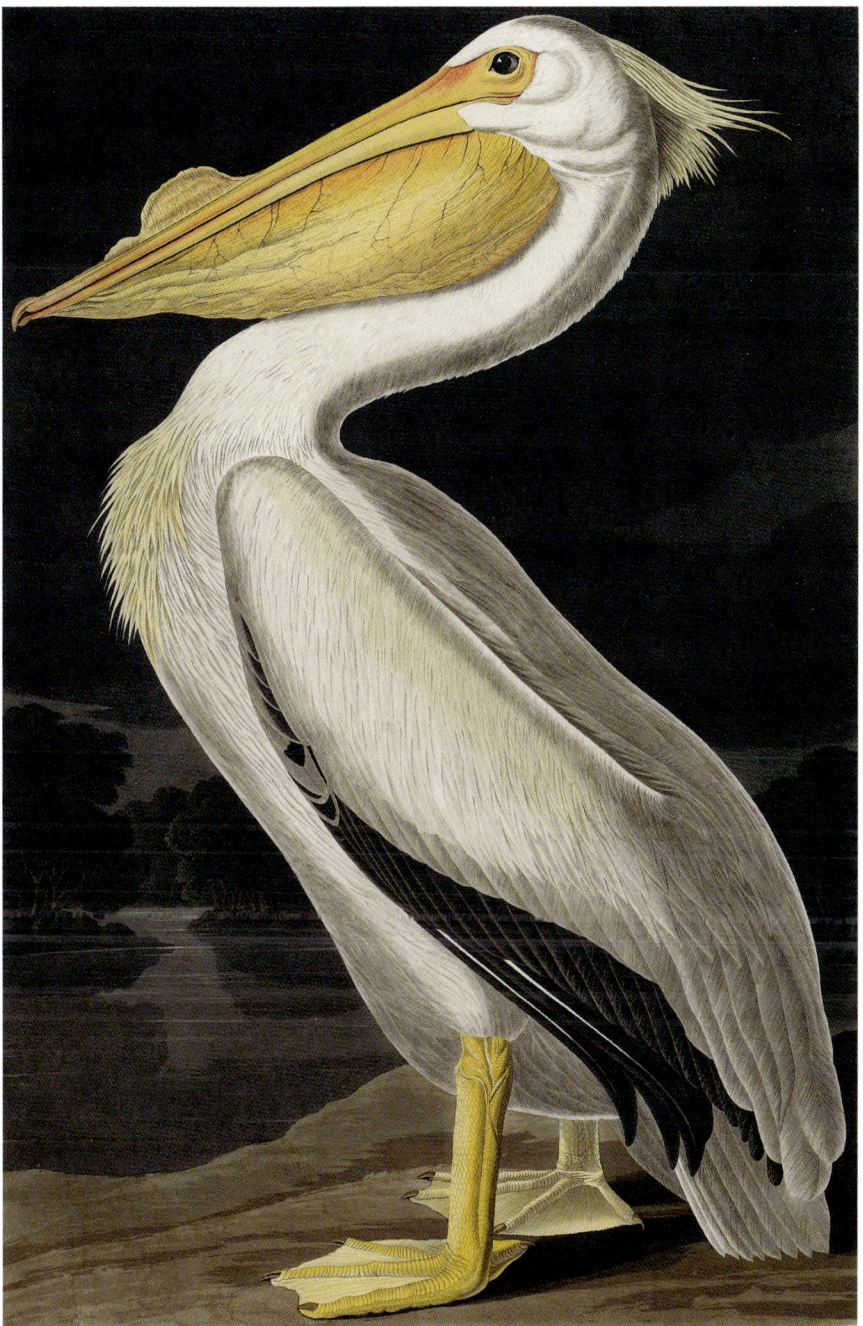

Wampum snake

Mark Catesby, *c.*1722–6

RCIN 926008

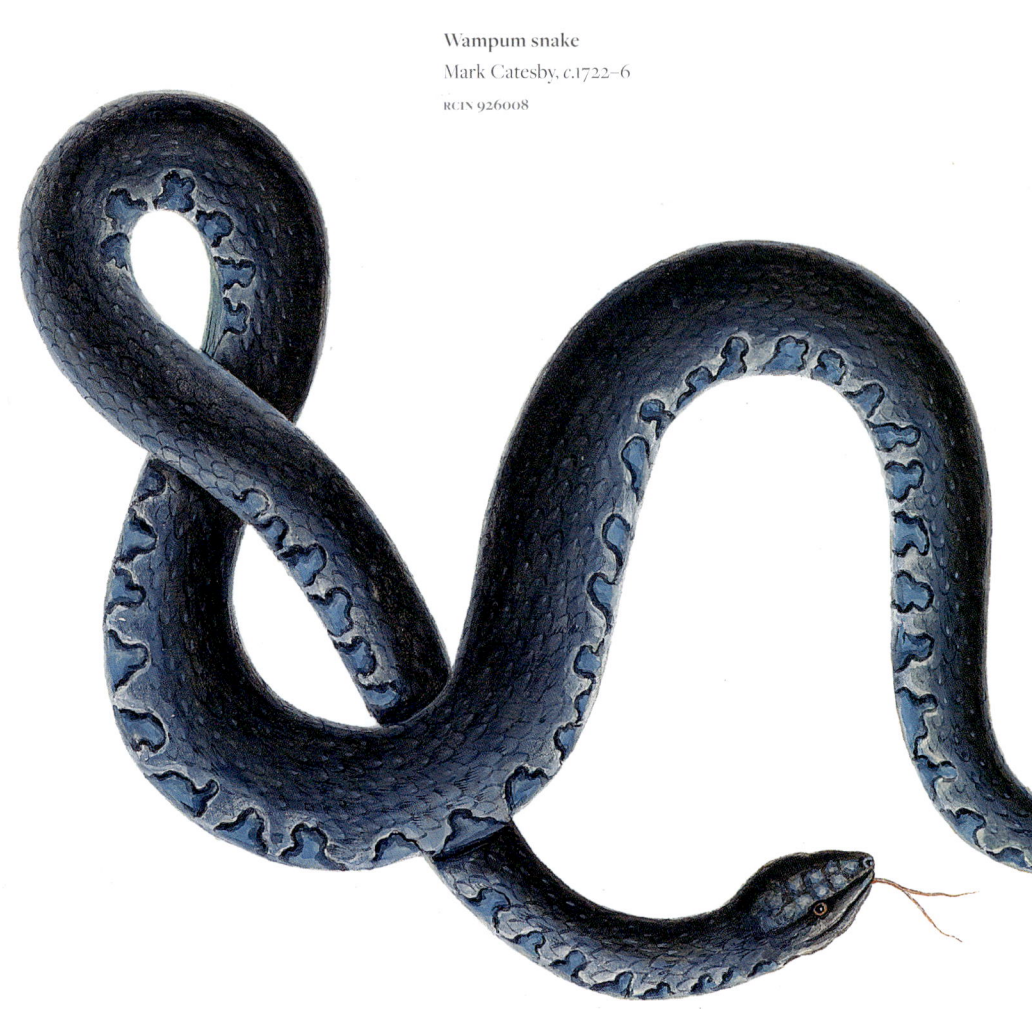

Blue-tailed sylph

From John Gould,
*A Monograph of the
Trochilidae, or family
of Humming-Birds,*
1861

RCIN 1055256

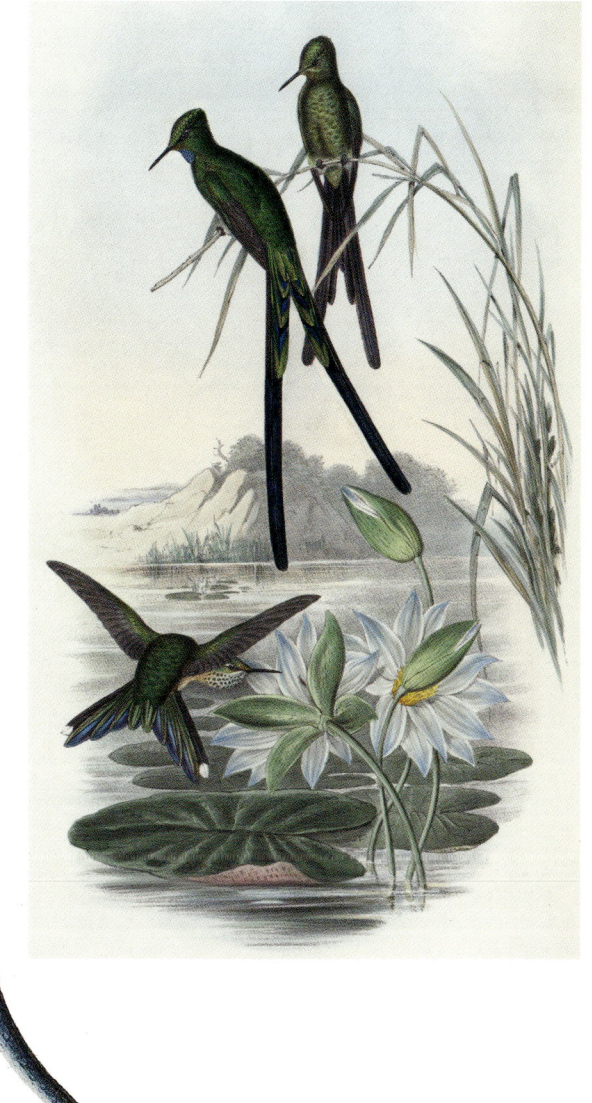

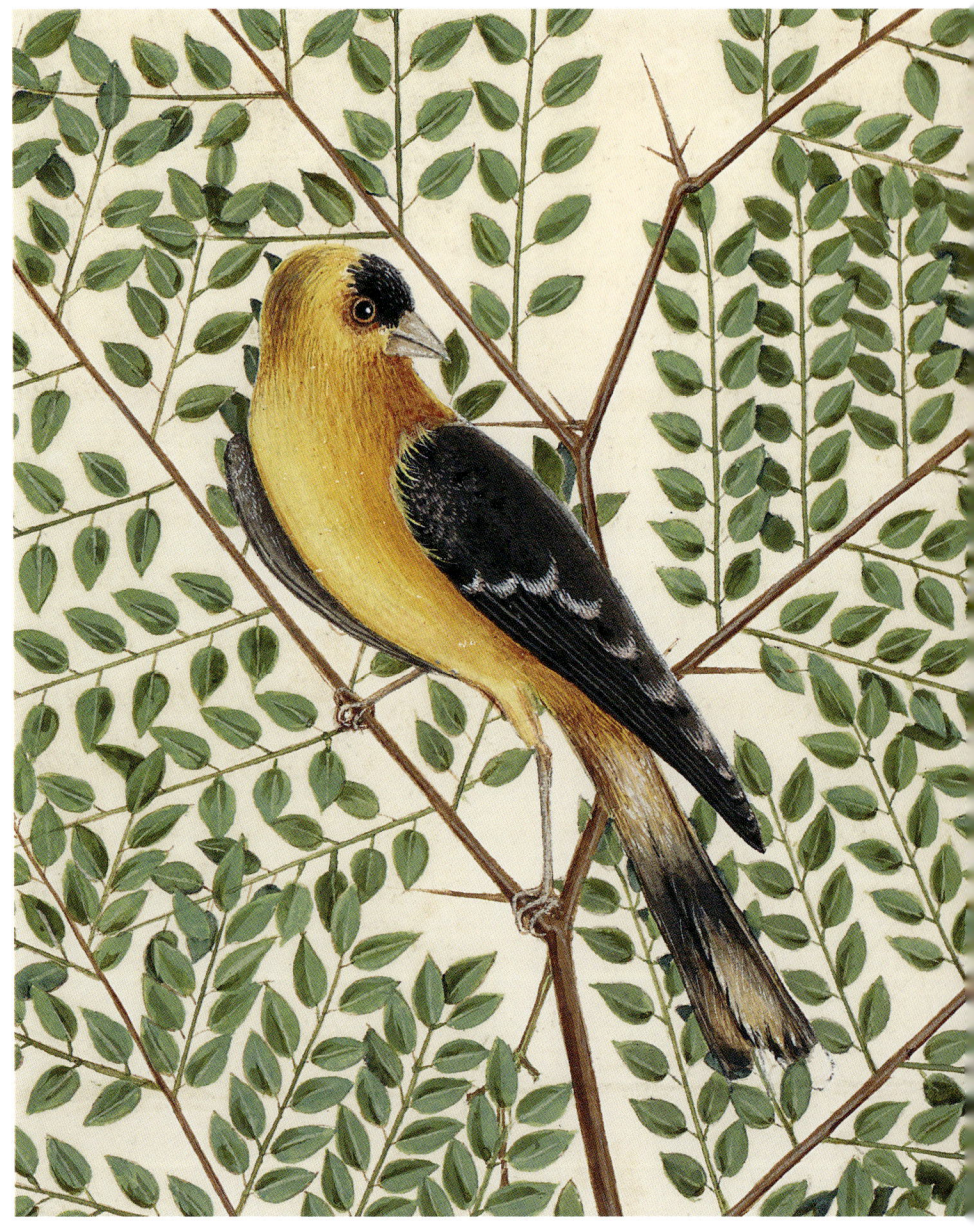

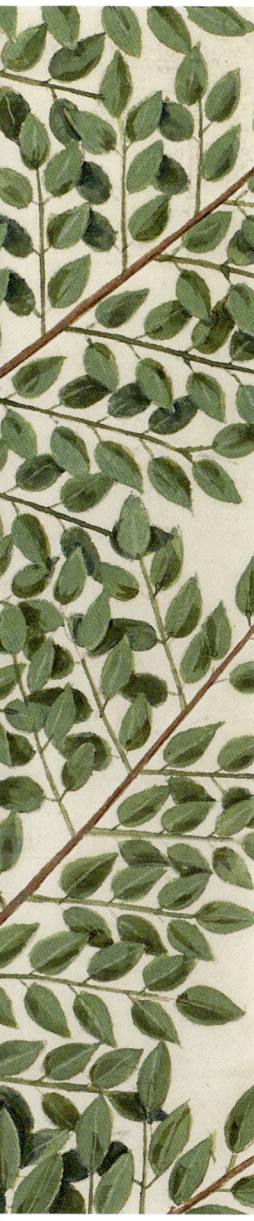

American goldfinch
and acacia (detail)

Mark Catesby,
c.1722–6

RCIN 924857

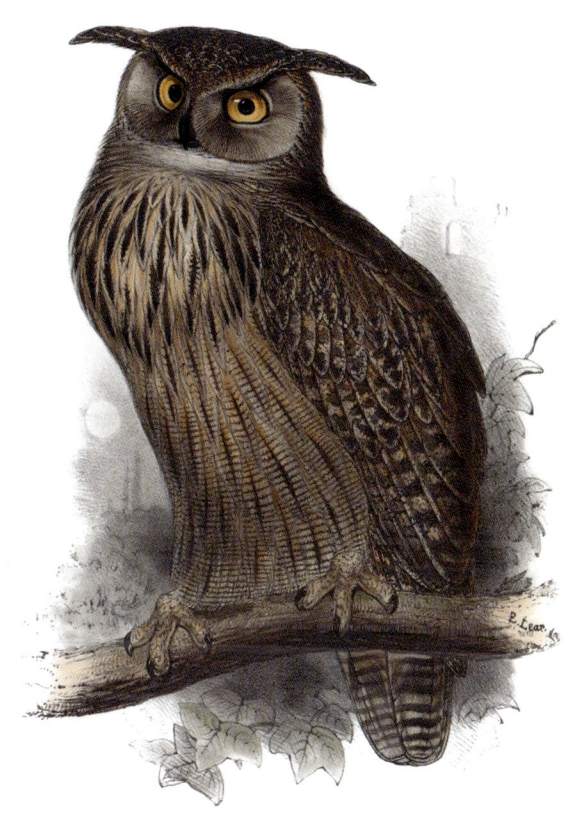

Eagle owl

From John Gould,
*The Birds of
Europe*, 1837

RCIN 1122367

North-Island brown kiwi

From Sir Walter Buller,
*A History of the Birds
of New Zealand*, 1873

RCIN 1057025

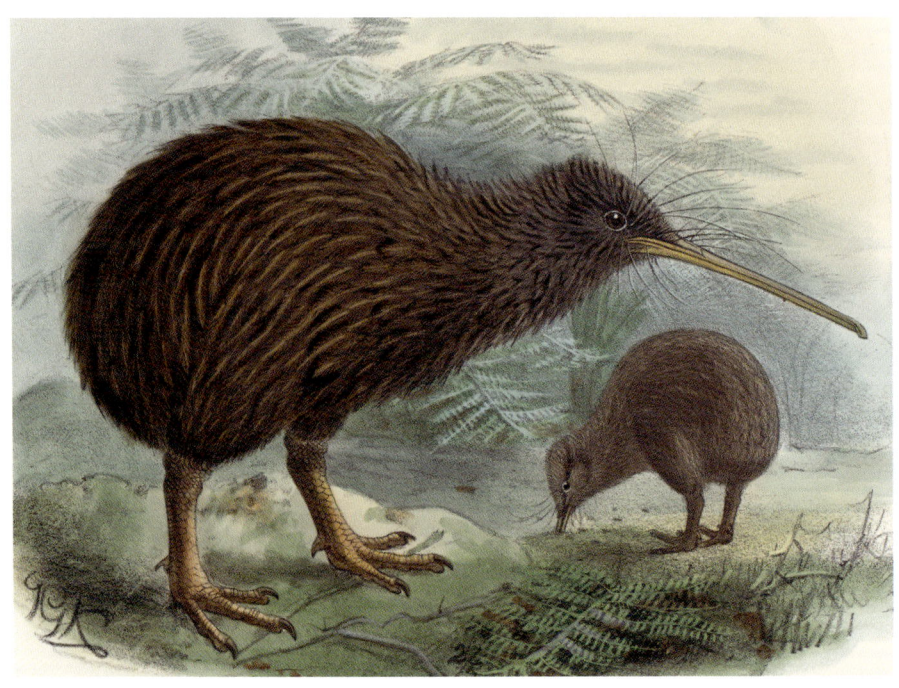

OPPOSITE

**Unadorned
rock wallaby**

From John Gould,
*The Mammals of
Australia*, 1863

RCIN 1122360

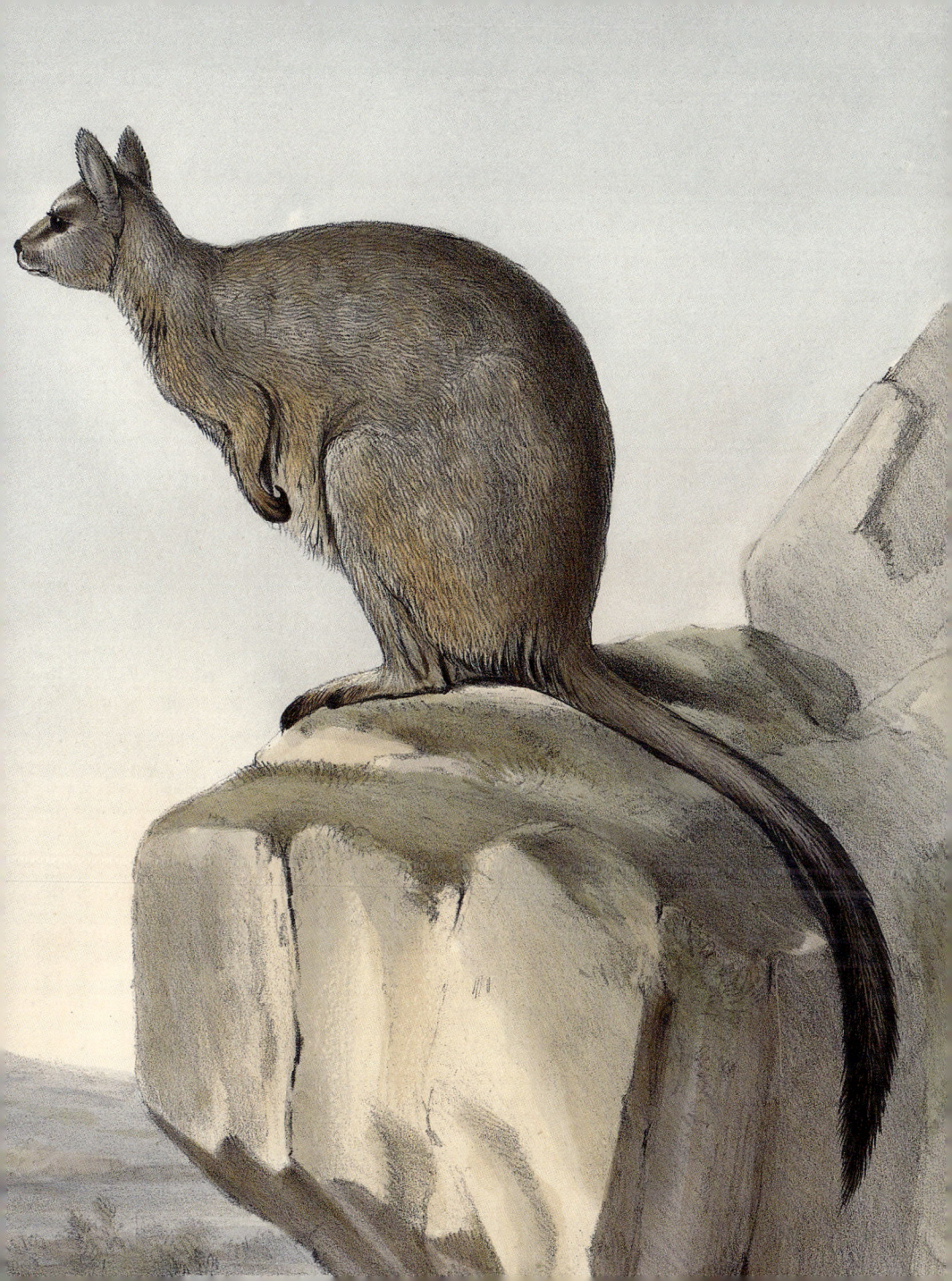

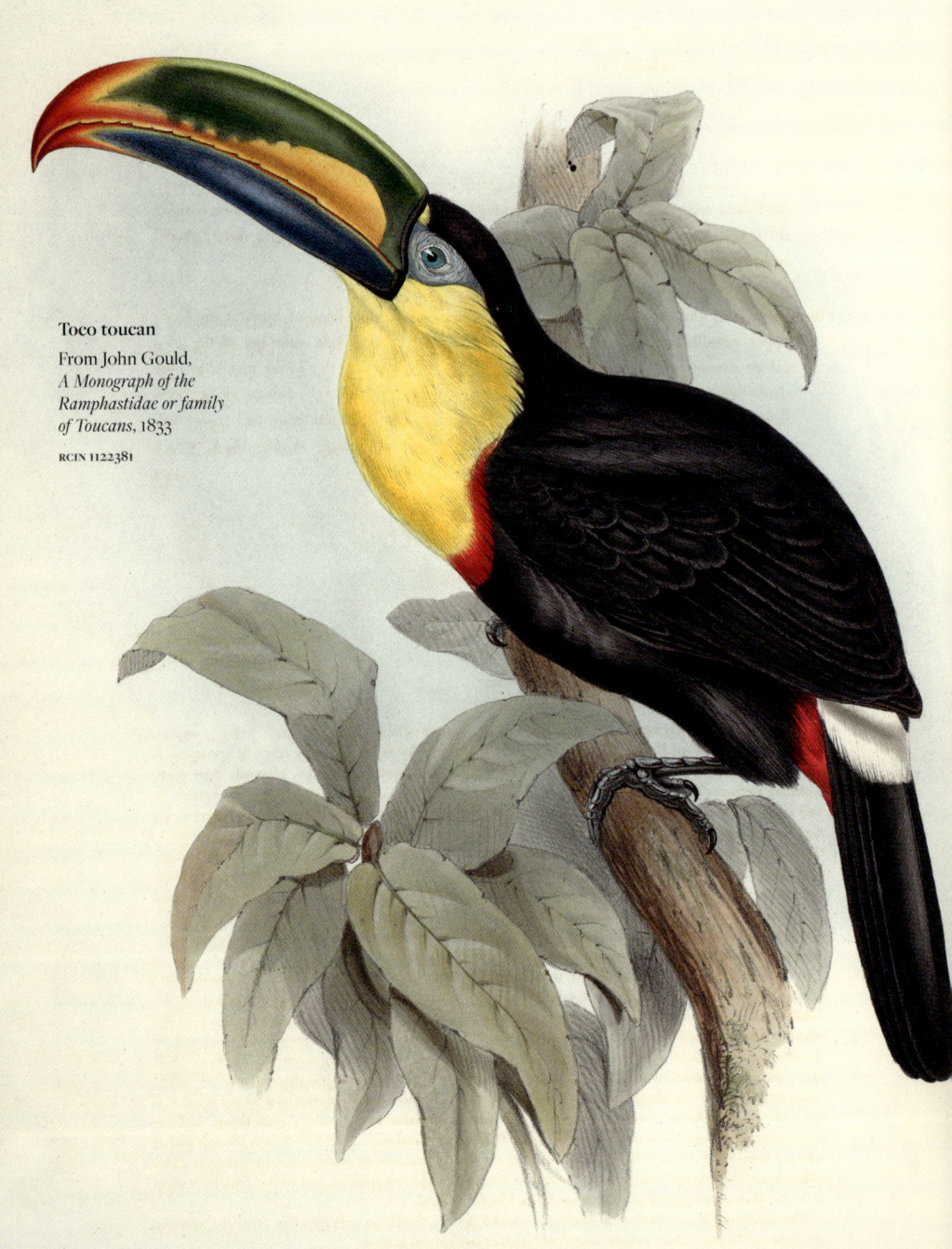

Toco toucan

From John Gould,
*A Monograph of the
Ramphastidae or family
of Toucans*, 1833

RCIN 1122381

TOP:

Rudder fish

BOTTOM:

Fresh-water pearch

Mark Catesby, *c.*1722–6

RCINs 925948–9

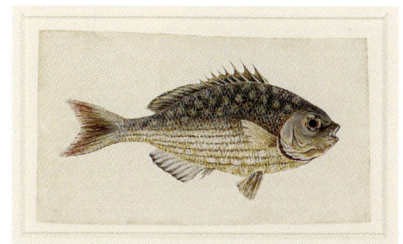

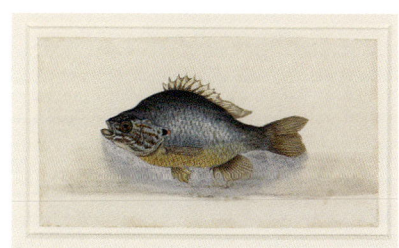

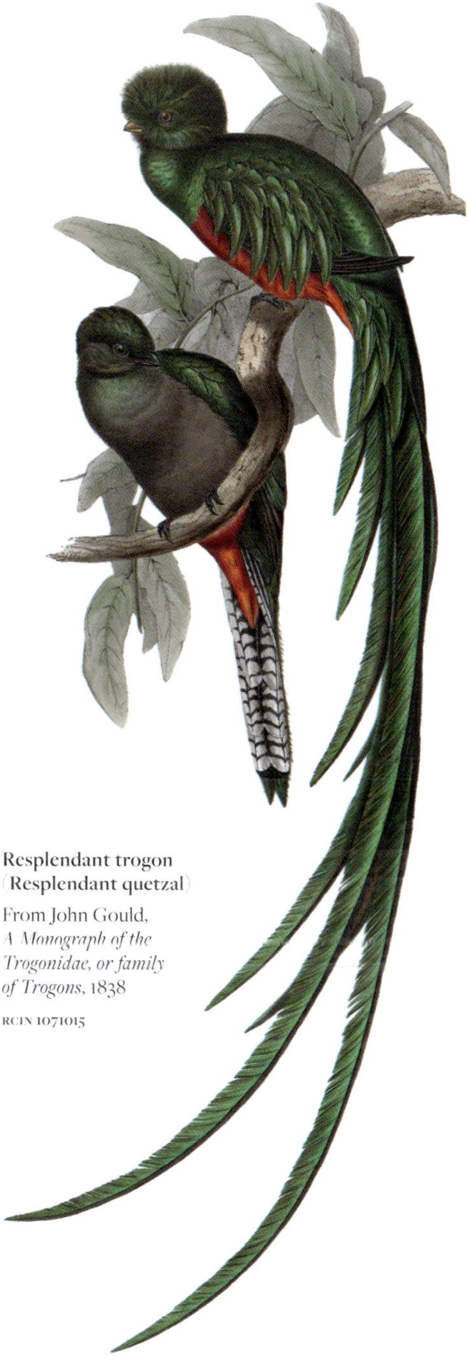

Resplendant trogon (Resplendant quetzal)

From John Gould,
*A Monograph of the
Trogonidae, or family
of Trogons,* 1838

RCIN 1071015

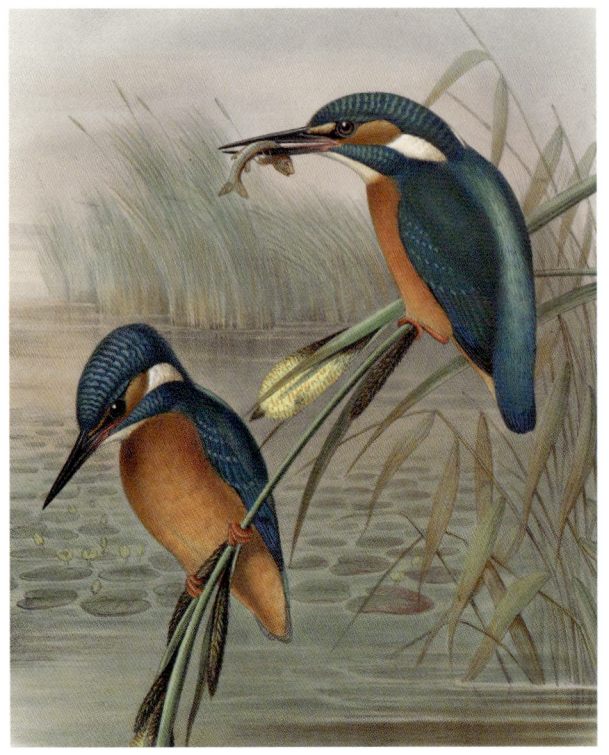

Kingfisher

From John Gould,
*The Birds of Great
Britain*, 1873

RCIN 1122343

OPPOSITE

Western tanager
and scarlet tanager

From John James
Audubon, *The Birds
of America*, 1836–8

RCIN 1122505

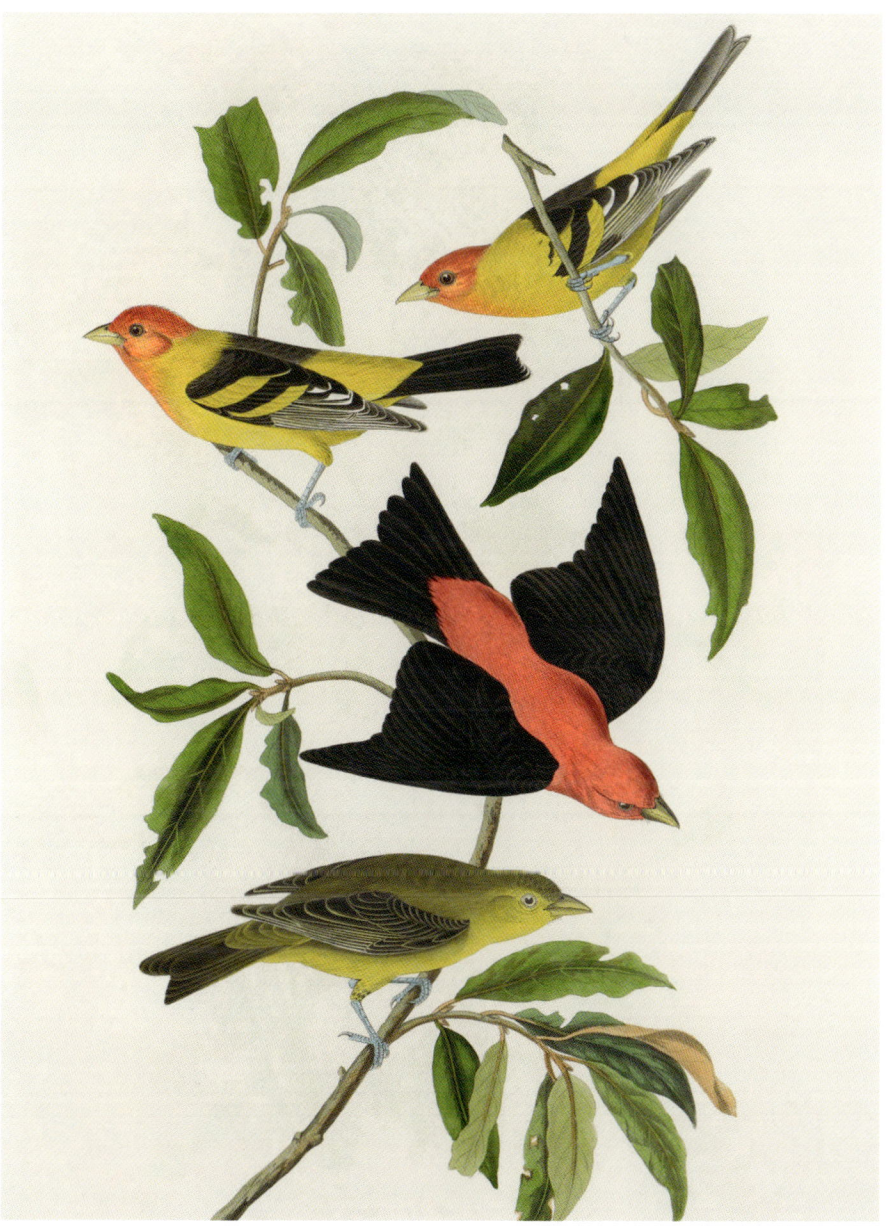

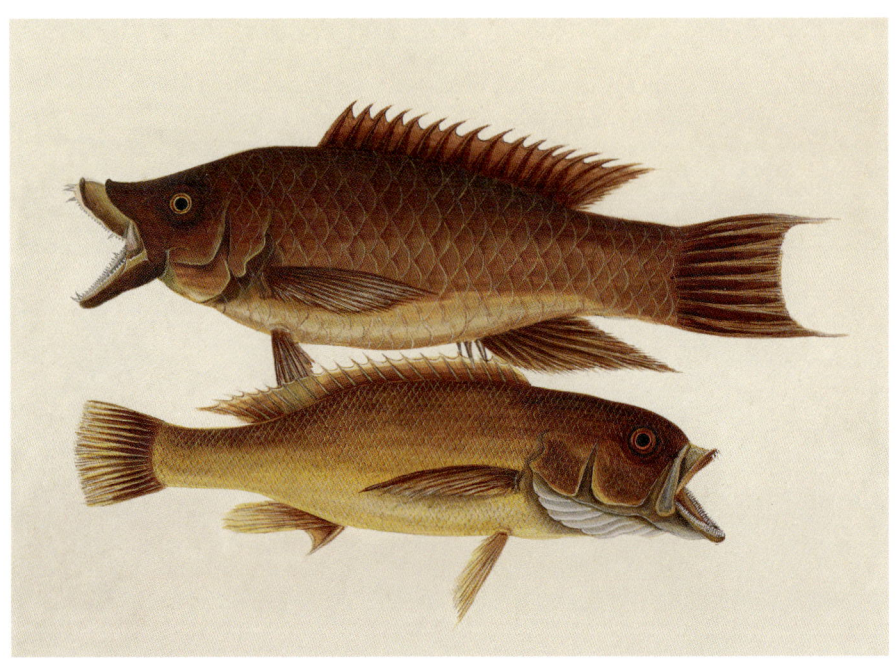

Yellow fish and hog fish

Mark Catesby, *c.*1722–6

RCIN 925952

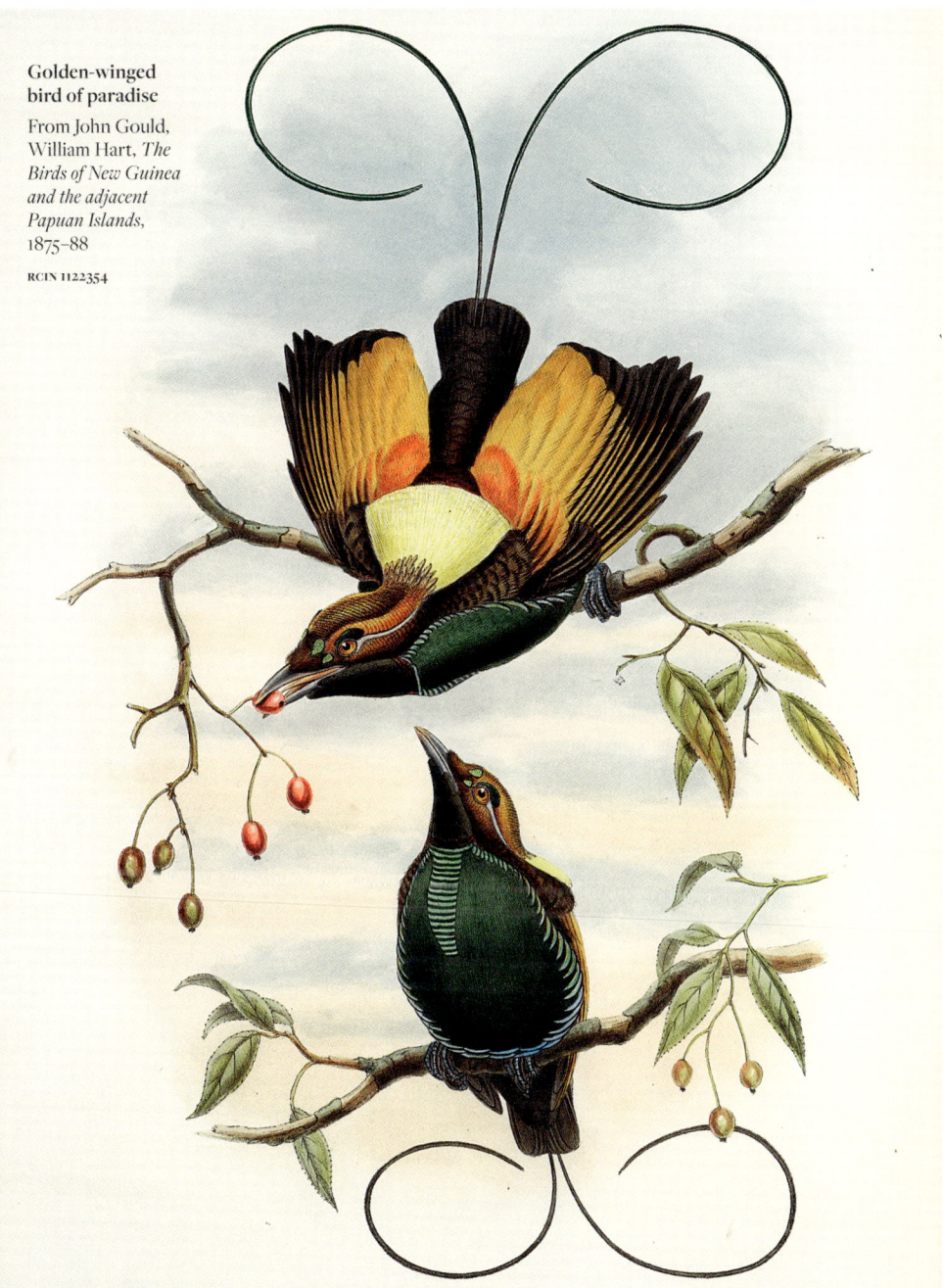

Golden-winged bird of paradise

From John Gould, William Hart, *The Birds of New Guinea and the adjacent Papuan Islands*, 1875–88

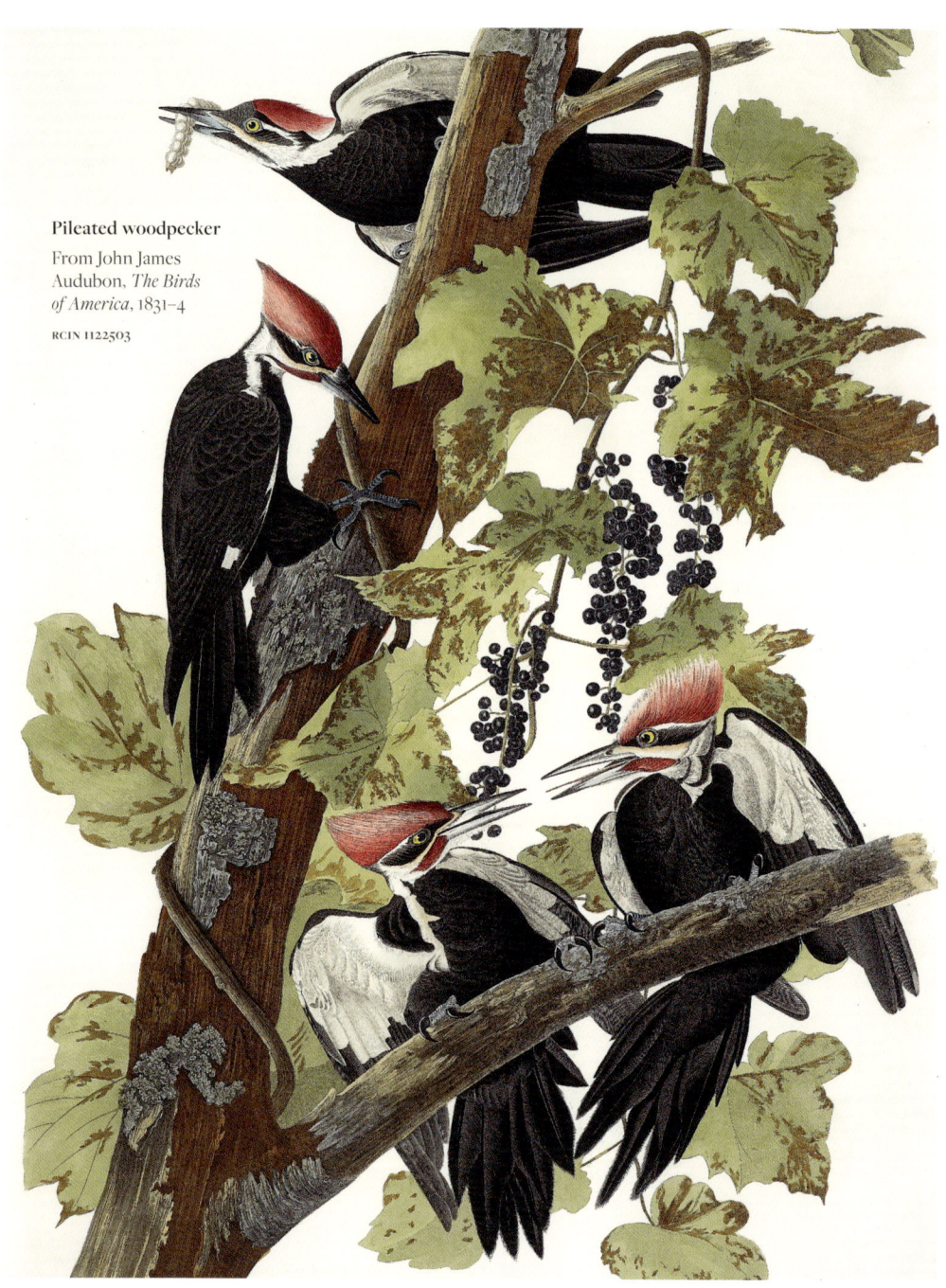

Pileated woodpecker

From John James
Audubon, *The Birds
of America*, 1831–4

RCIN 1122503

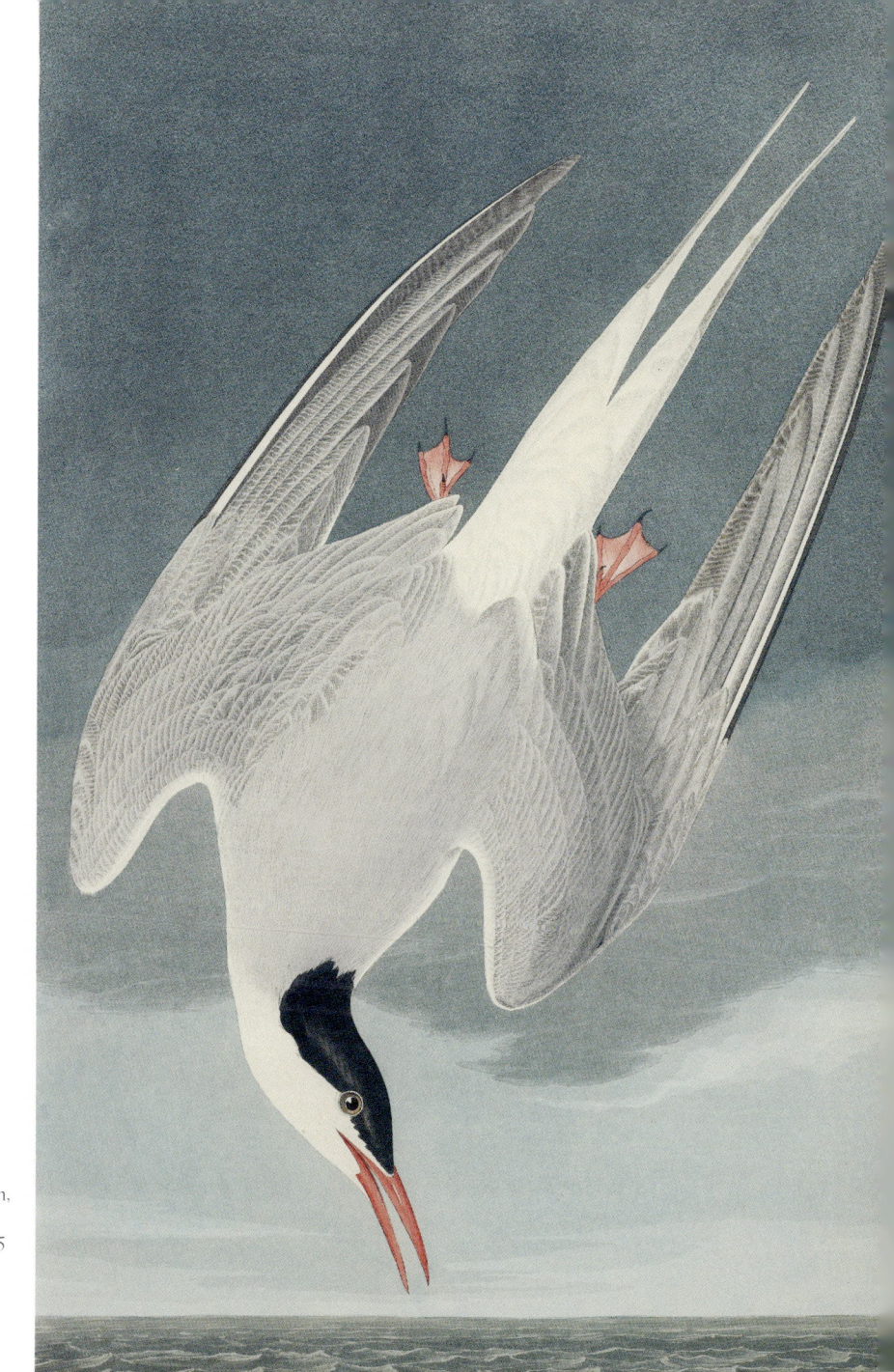

Arctic tern

From John
James Audubon,
*The Birds of
America*, 1834–5

Golden tegu lizard

Maria Sibylla Merian,
c.1705–10

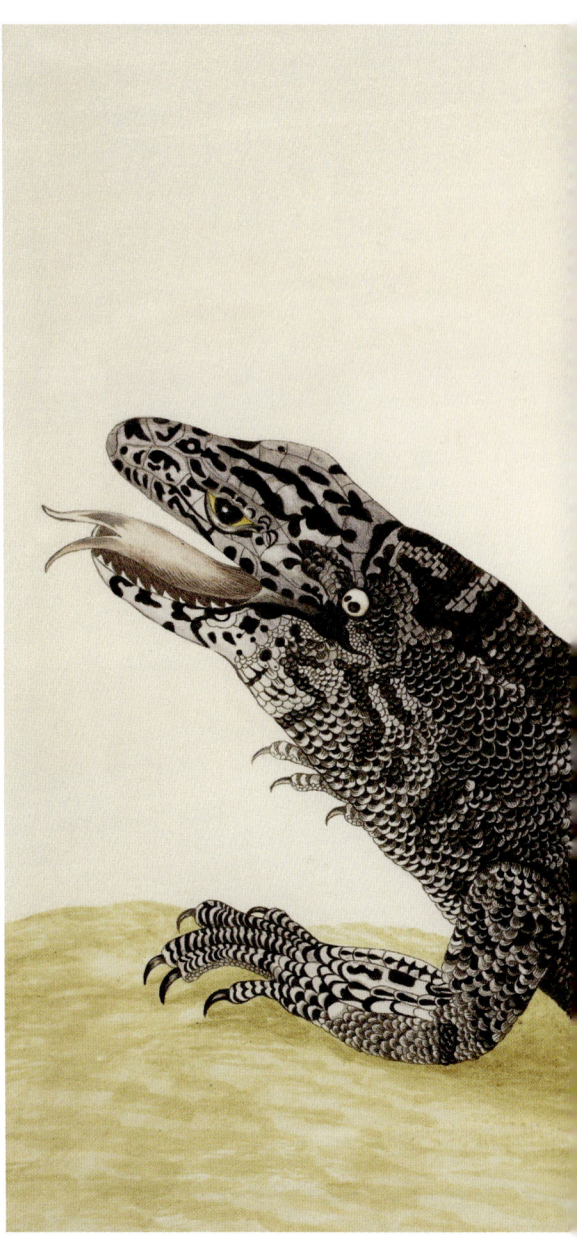

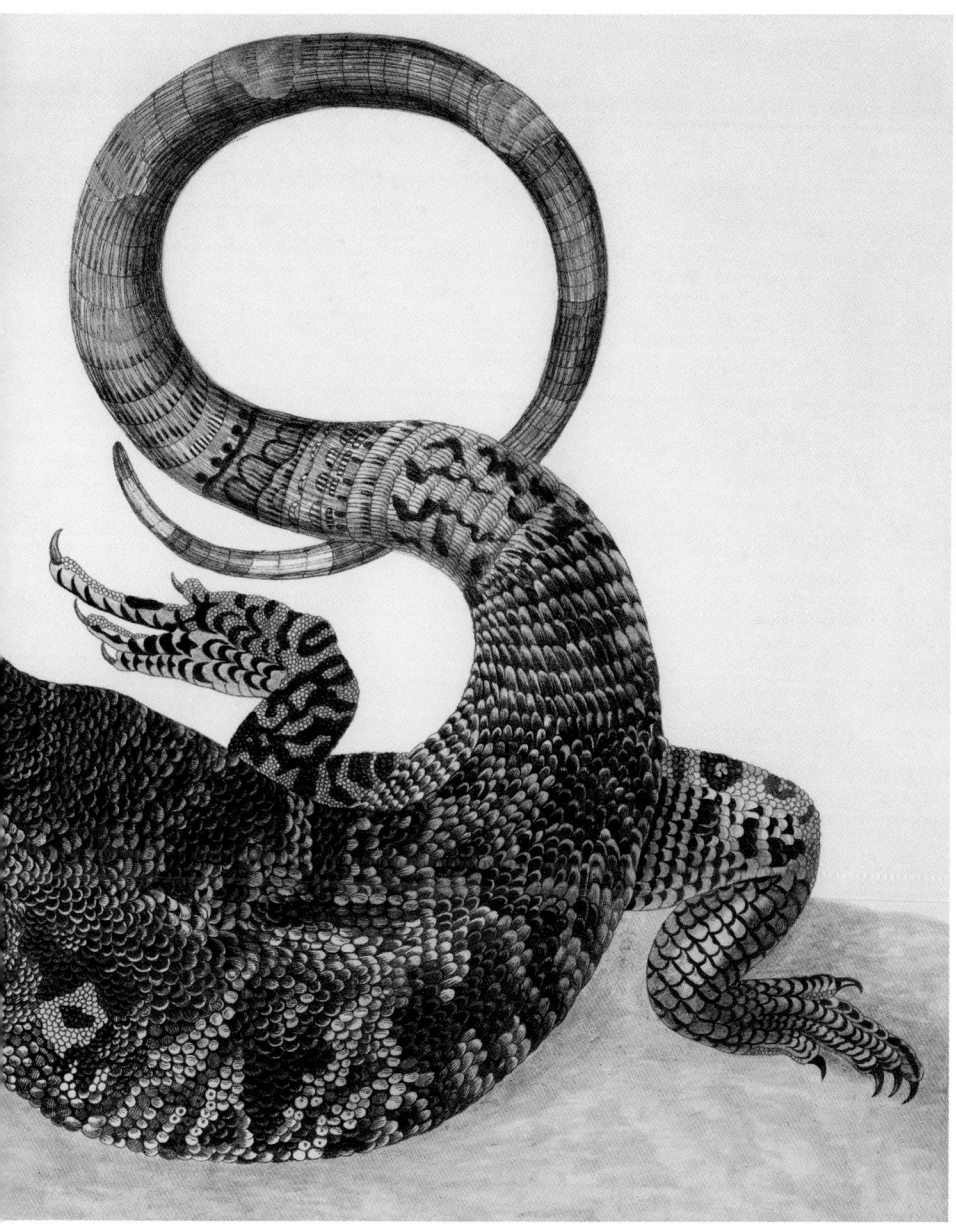

OPPOSITE

Gyrfalcon

From John James
Audubon, *The Birds
of America*, 1836–8

RCIN 1122505

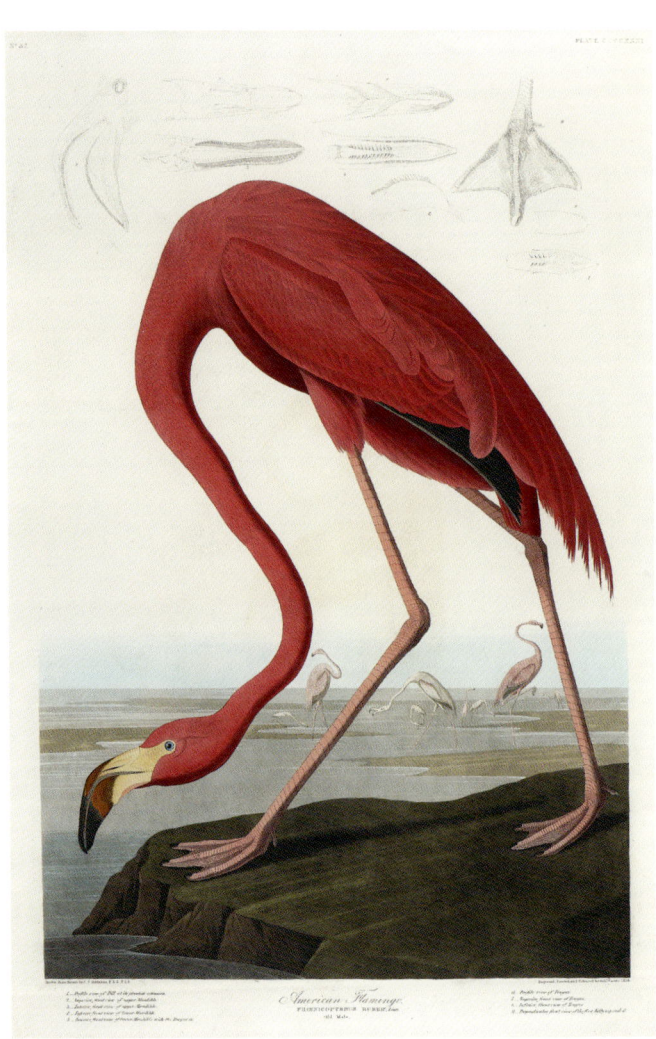

American flamingo

John James Audubon,
The Birds of America,
1836–8

RCIN 1122505

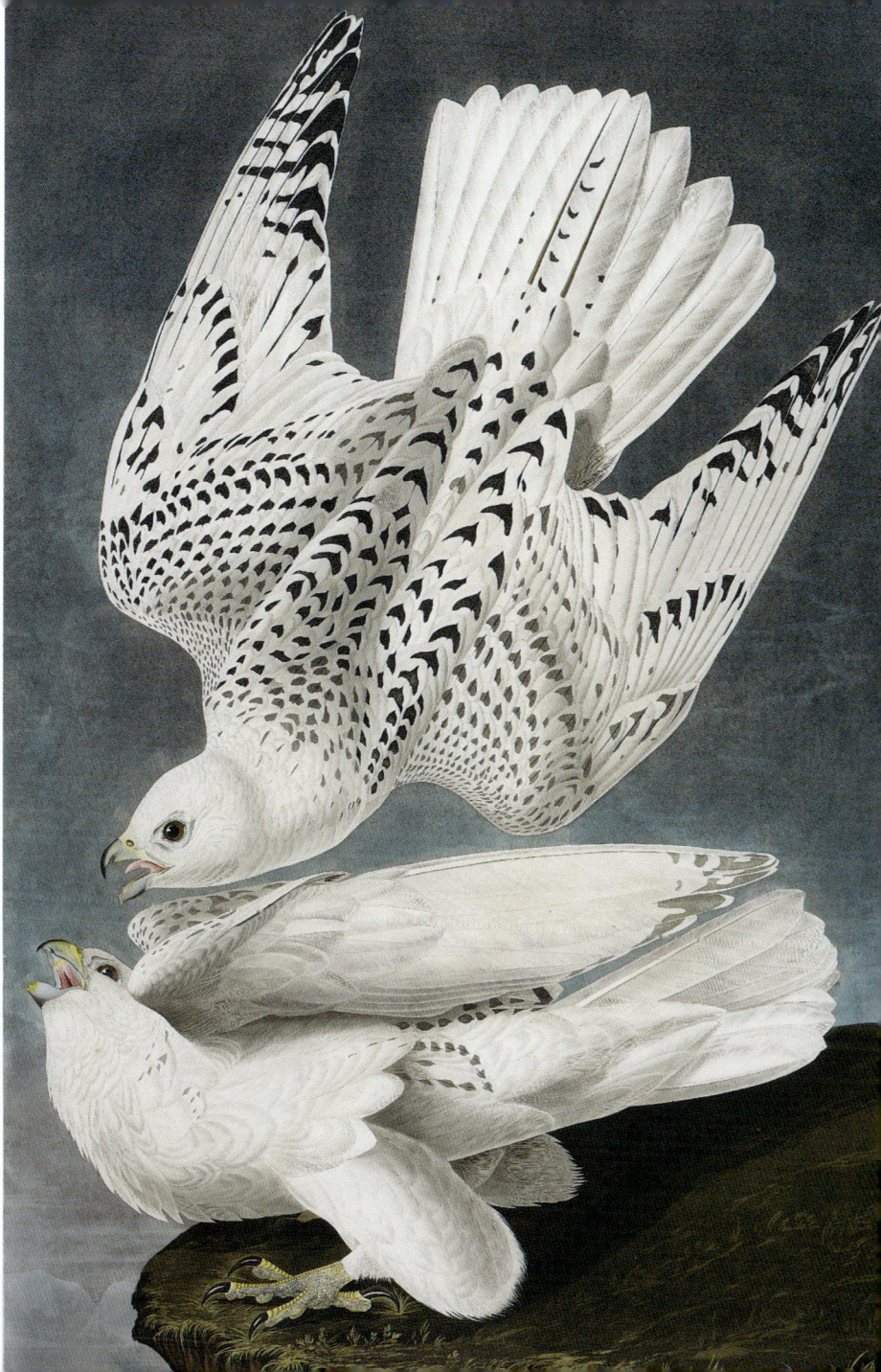

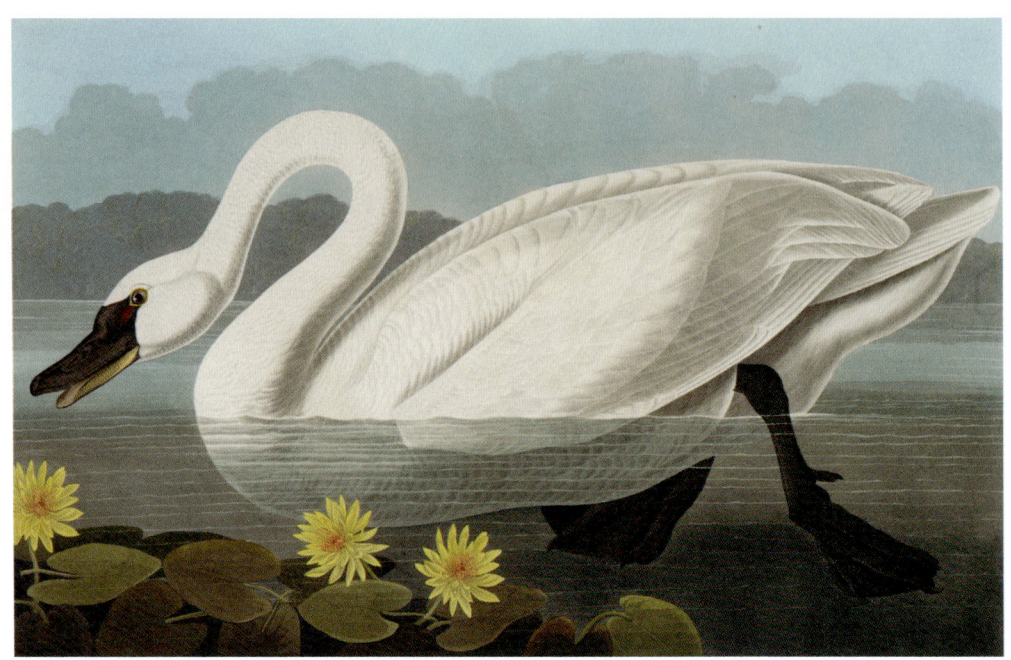

Tundra swan

From John James
Audubon, *The Birds
of America*, 1836–8

RCIN 1122505

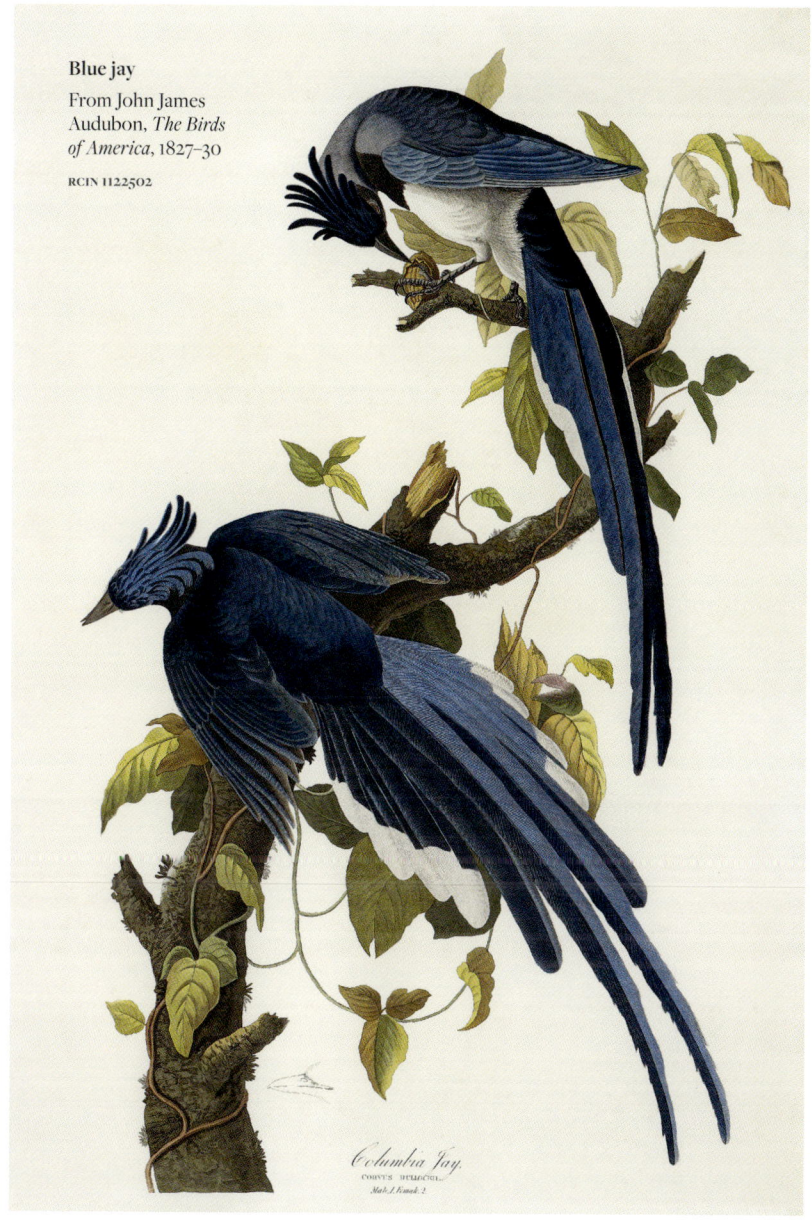

Blue jay

From John James
Audubon, *The Birds
of America*, 1827–30

RCIN 1122502

Columbia Jay,
CORVUS BULLOCKII.
Male 1. Female 2.

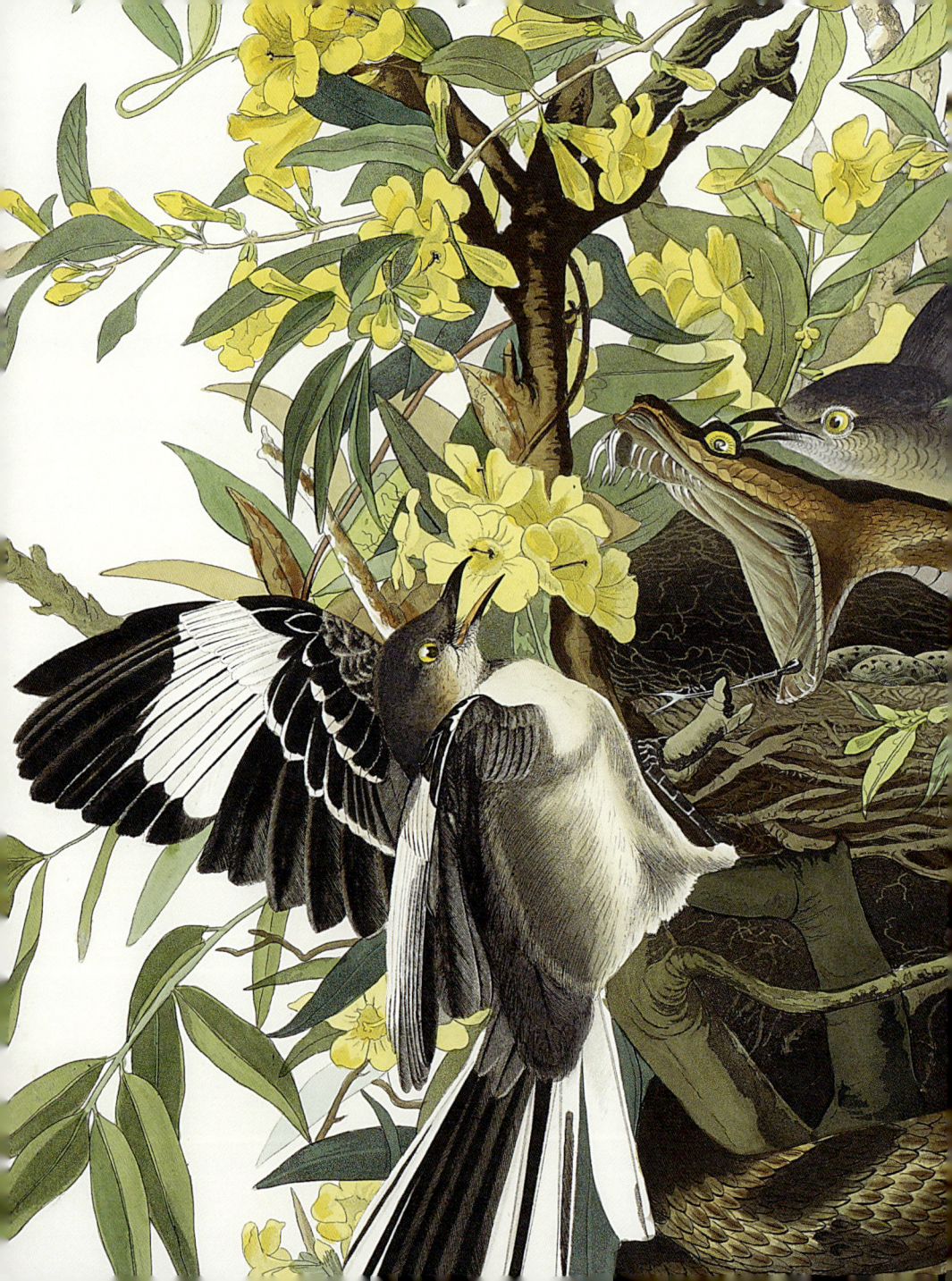

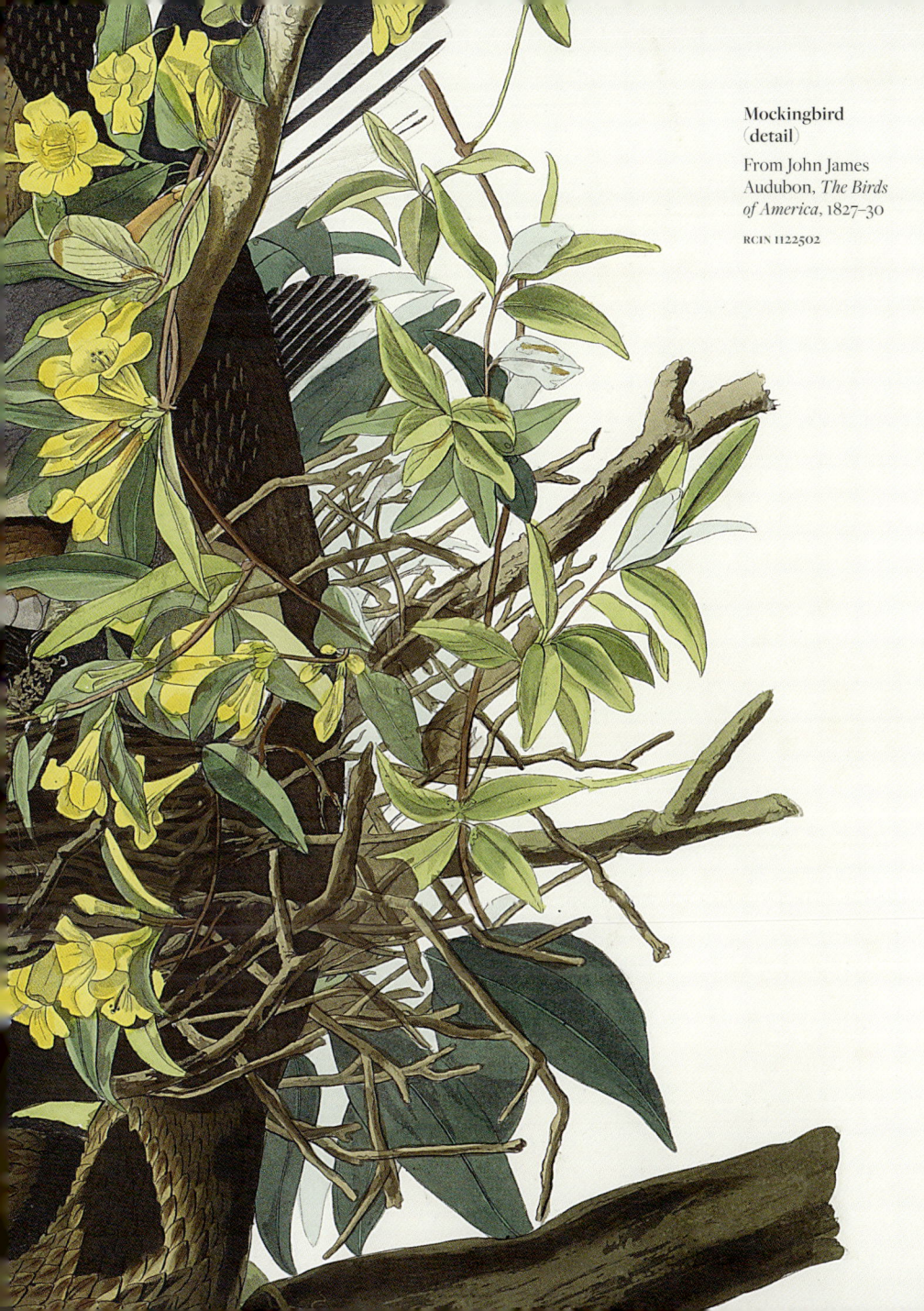

Mockingbird
(detail)

From John James
Audubon, *The Birds
of America*, 1827–30

RCIN 1122502

OPPOSITE

Red bird

Mark Catesby,
*c.*1722–6

RCIN 924852

Rattle-snake

Mark Catesby,
*c.*1722–6

RCIN 925987

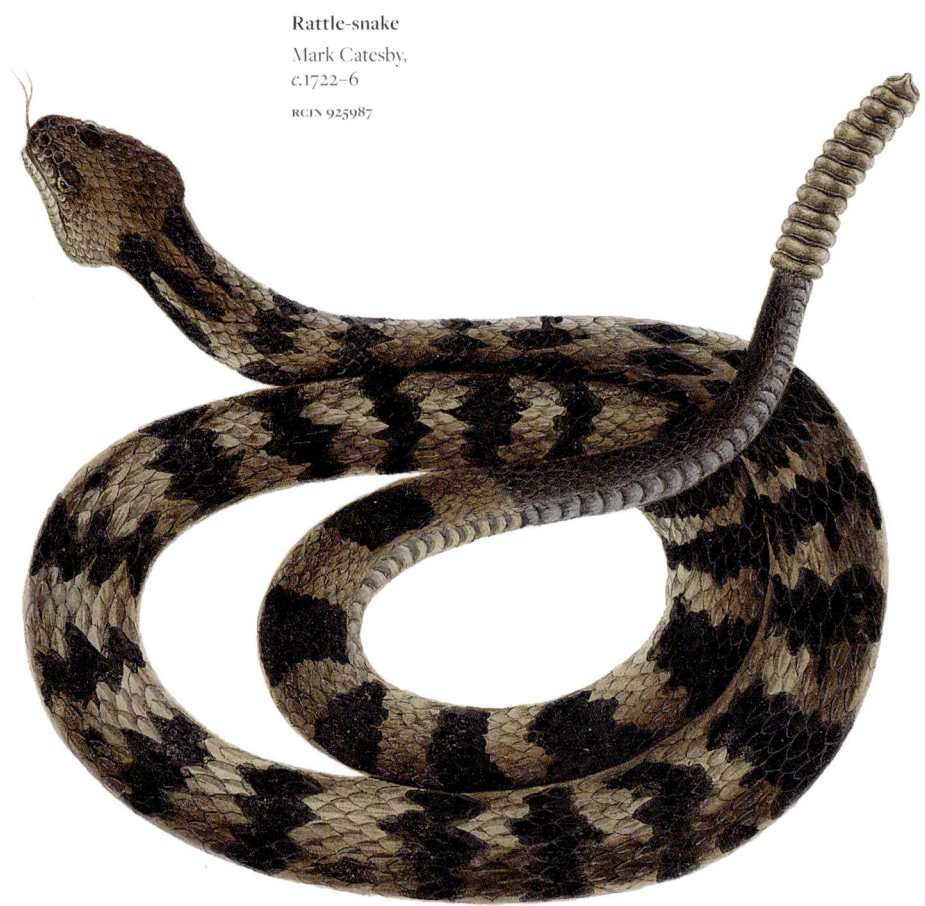

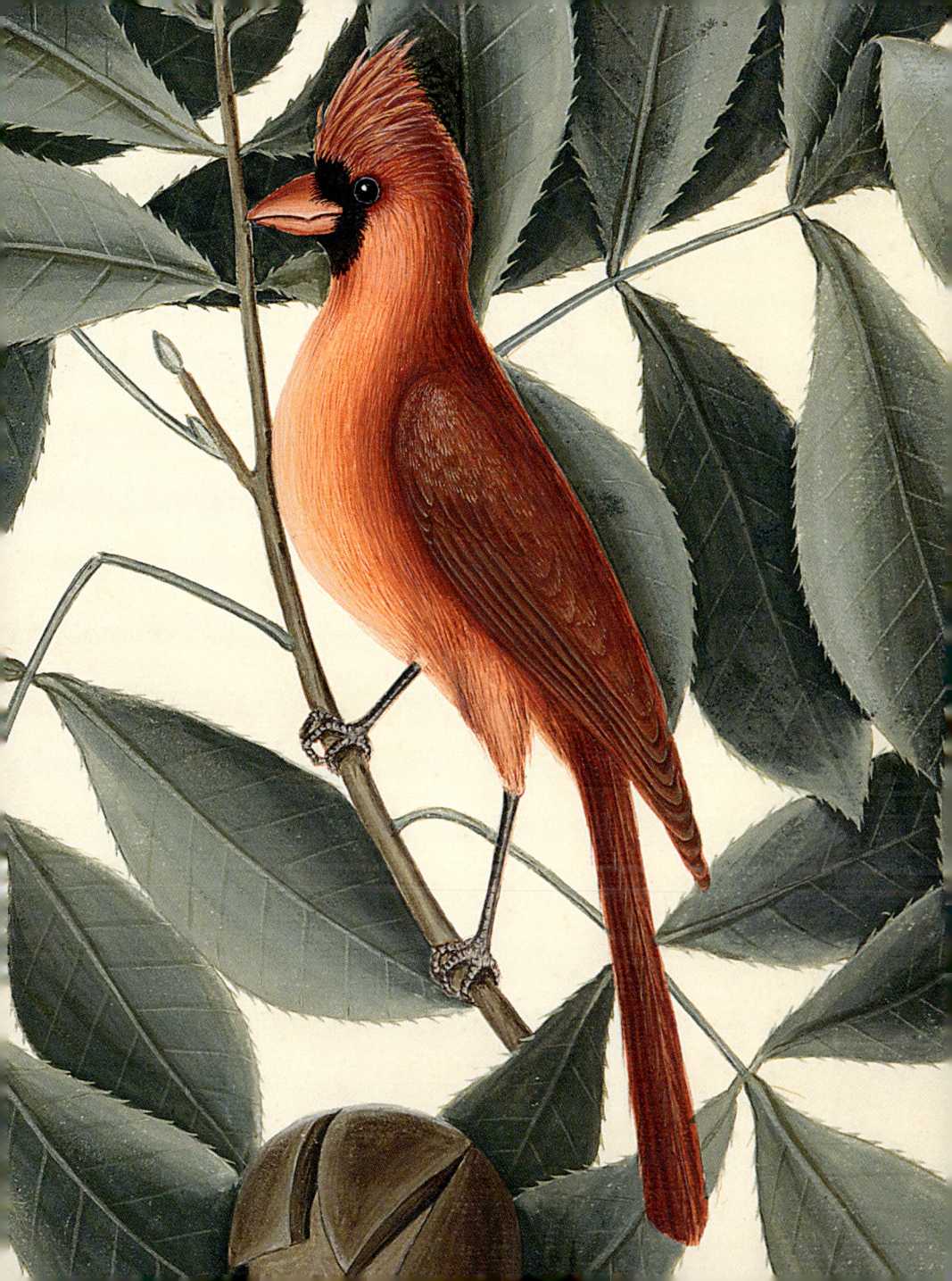

Garden tree boa, rustic
sphinx moth and treehopper

Maria Sybilla Merian, 1702–3

RCIN 921159

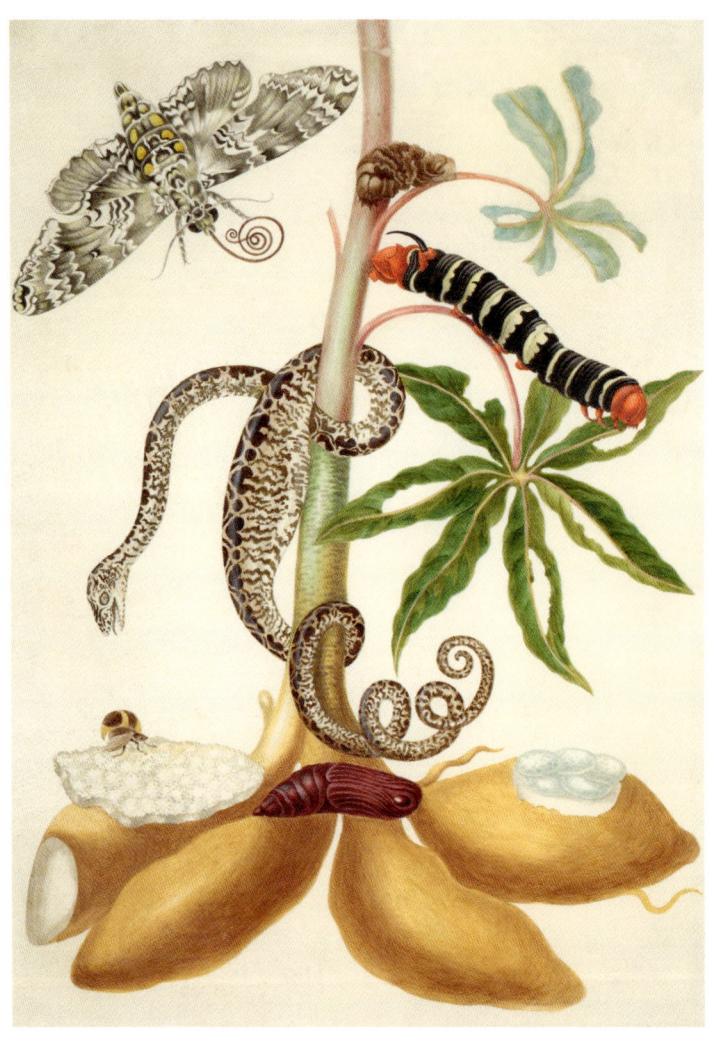

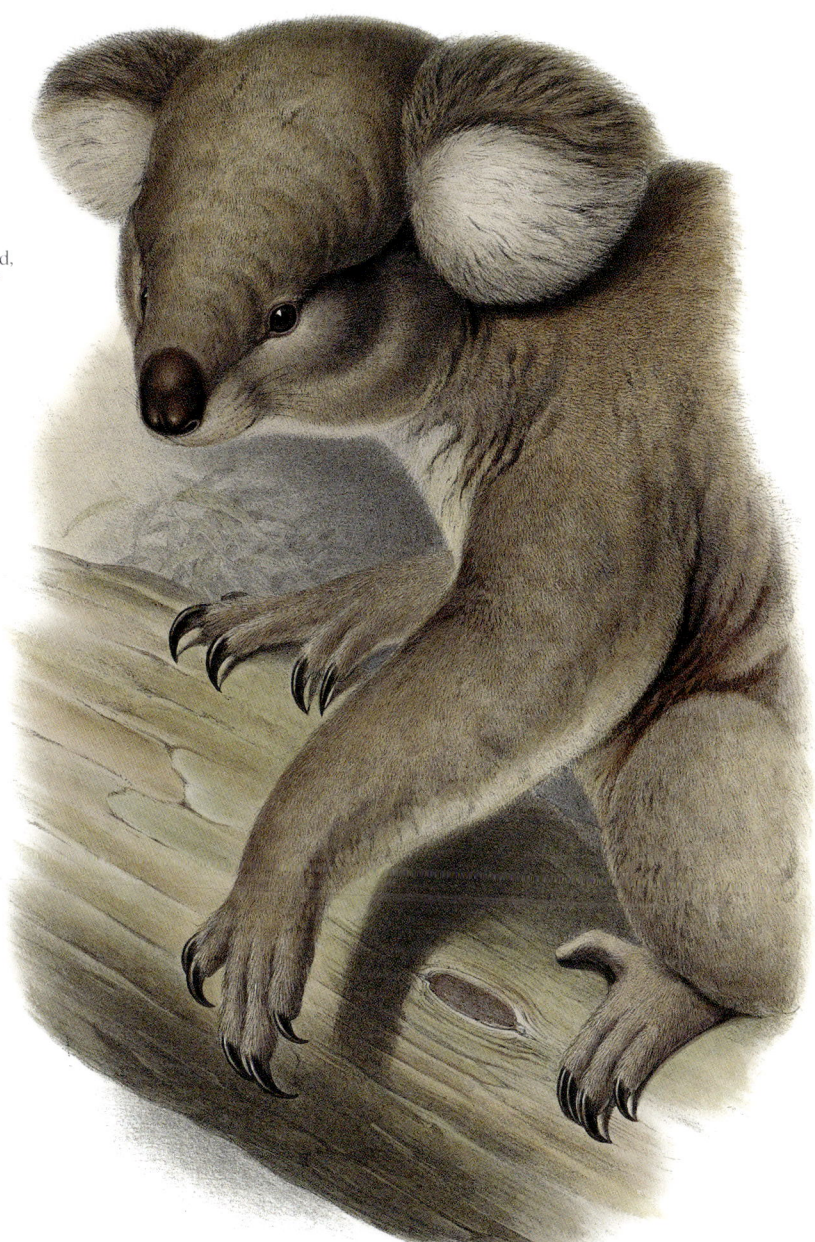

Koala

From John Gould,
*The Mammals of
Australia*, 1863

RCIN 1122359

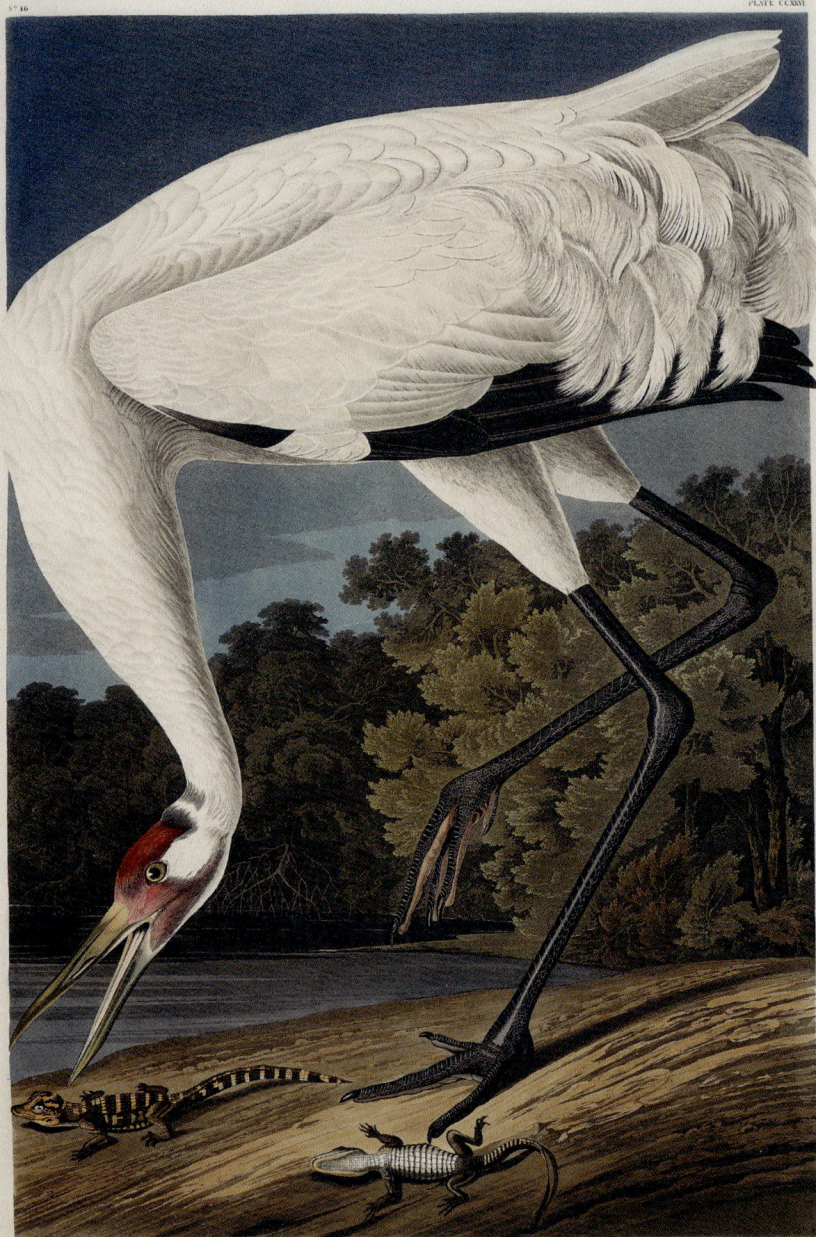

Hooping Crane. GRUS AMERICANA. *Adult Male.*

Hooping crane

From John James
Audubon, *The Birds
of America*, 1834–5

RCIN 1122504

Puffin

From John James
Audubon, *The Birds
of America*, 1834–5

RCIN 1122504

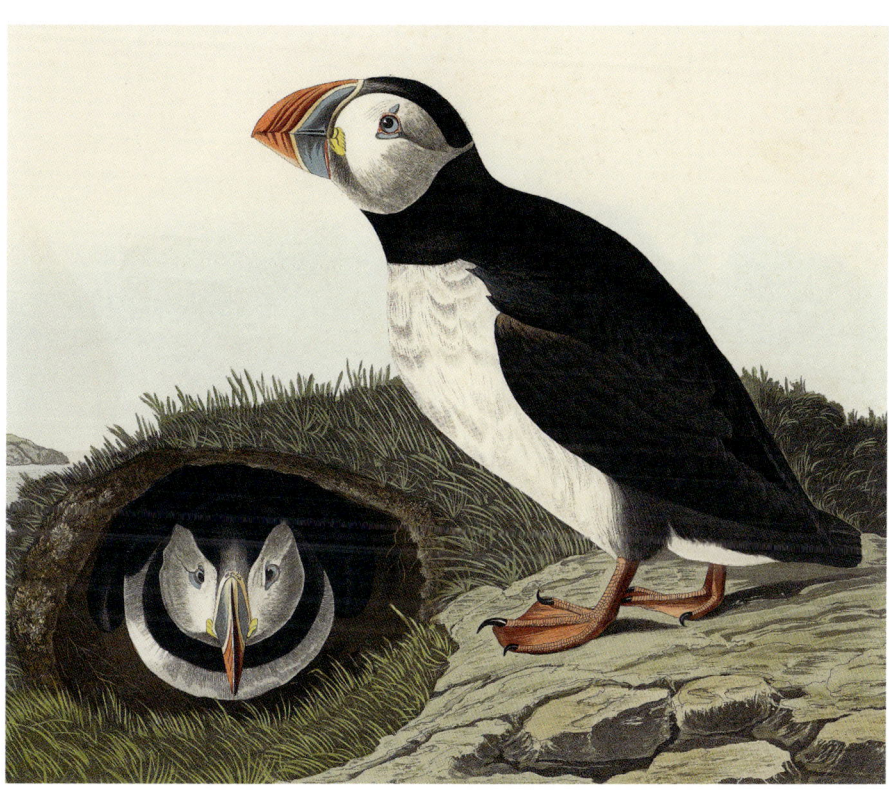

Vitoe (Feline night monkey)

From Edward Lear, *Gleanings from the Menagerie and Aviary at Knowsley Hall*, 1846–50

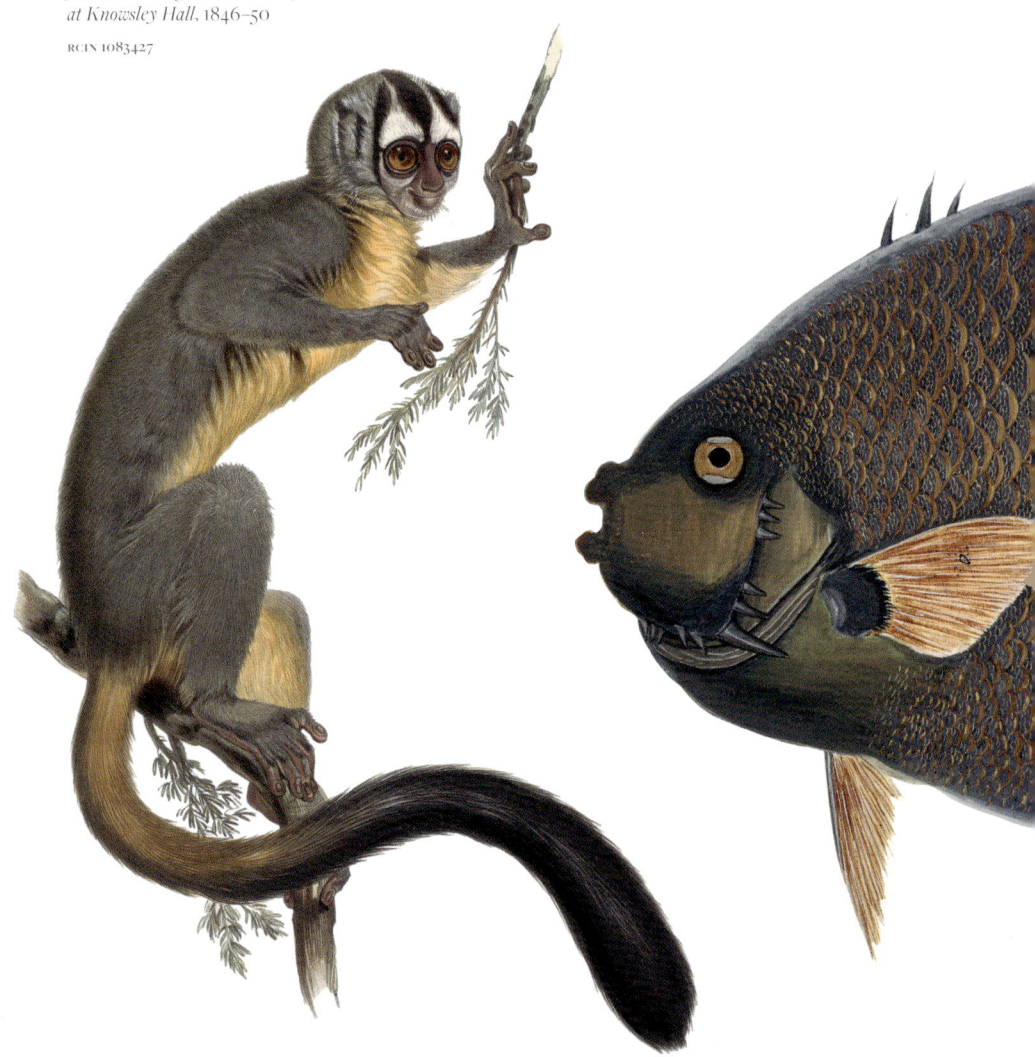

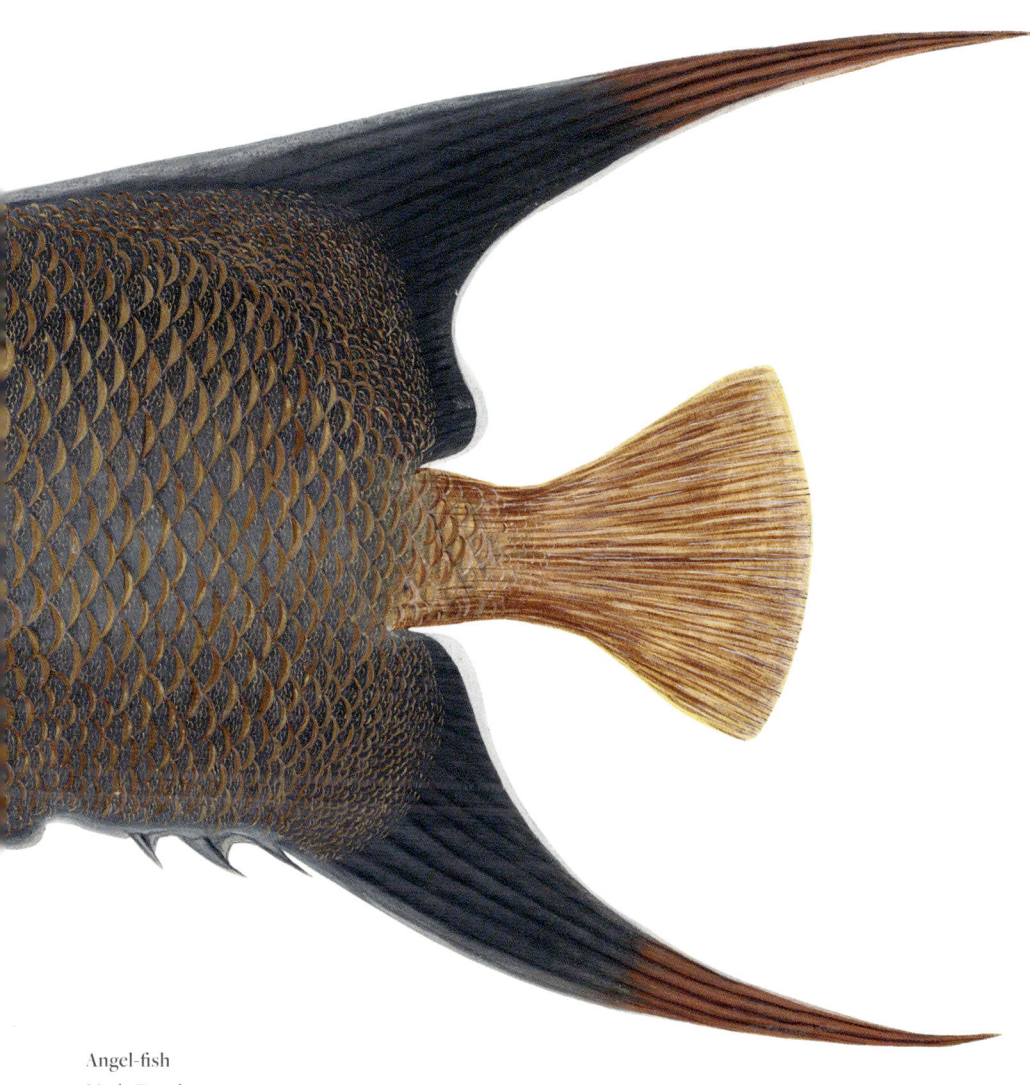

Angel-fish

Mark Catesby,
c.1722–6

RCIN 925976

**Menelaus blue
morpho butterfly**

Maria Sibylla
Merian, 1705

RCIN 1085787

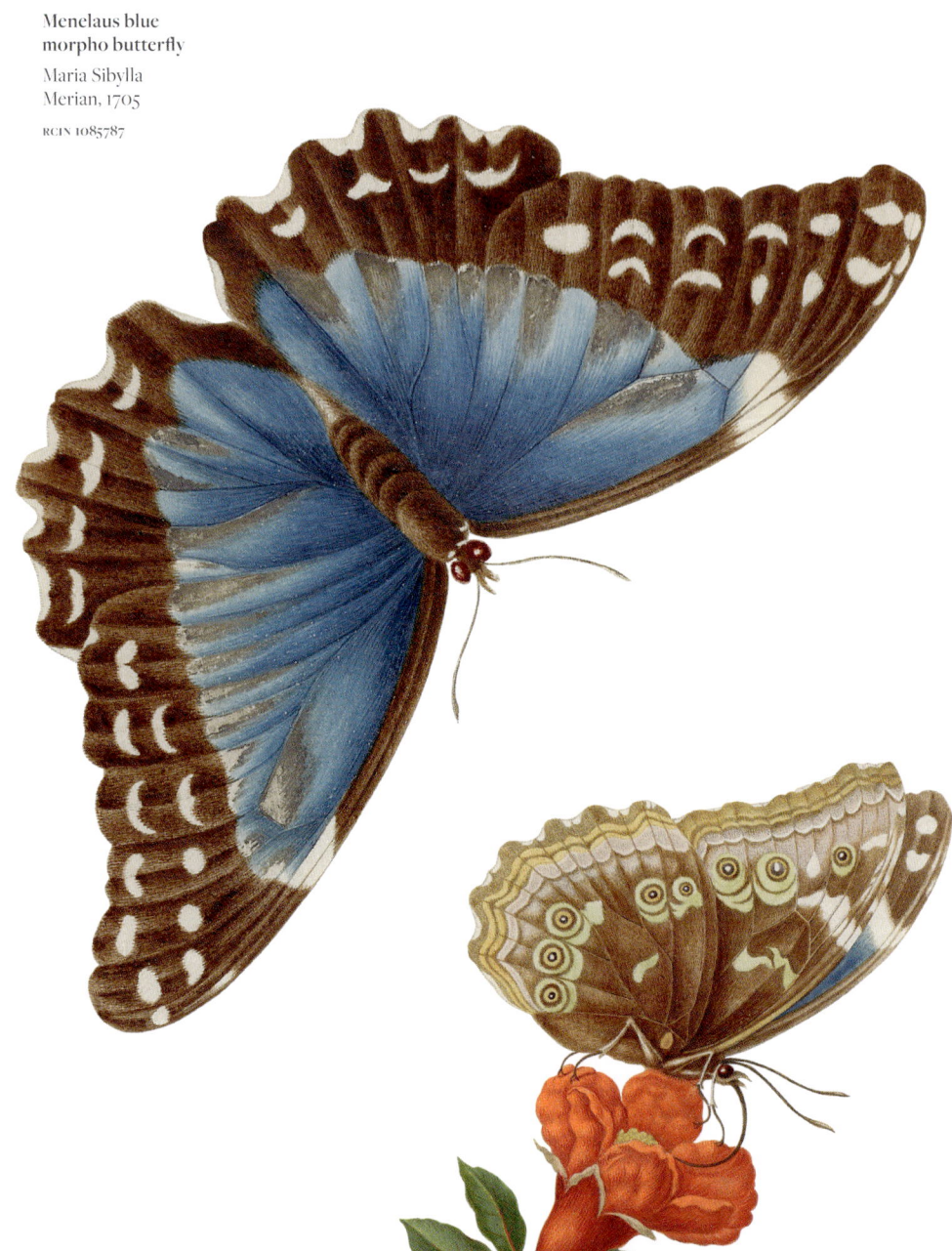

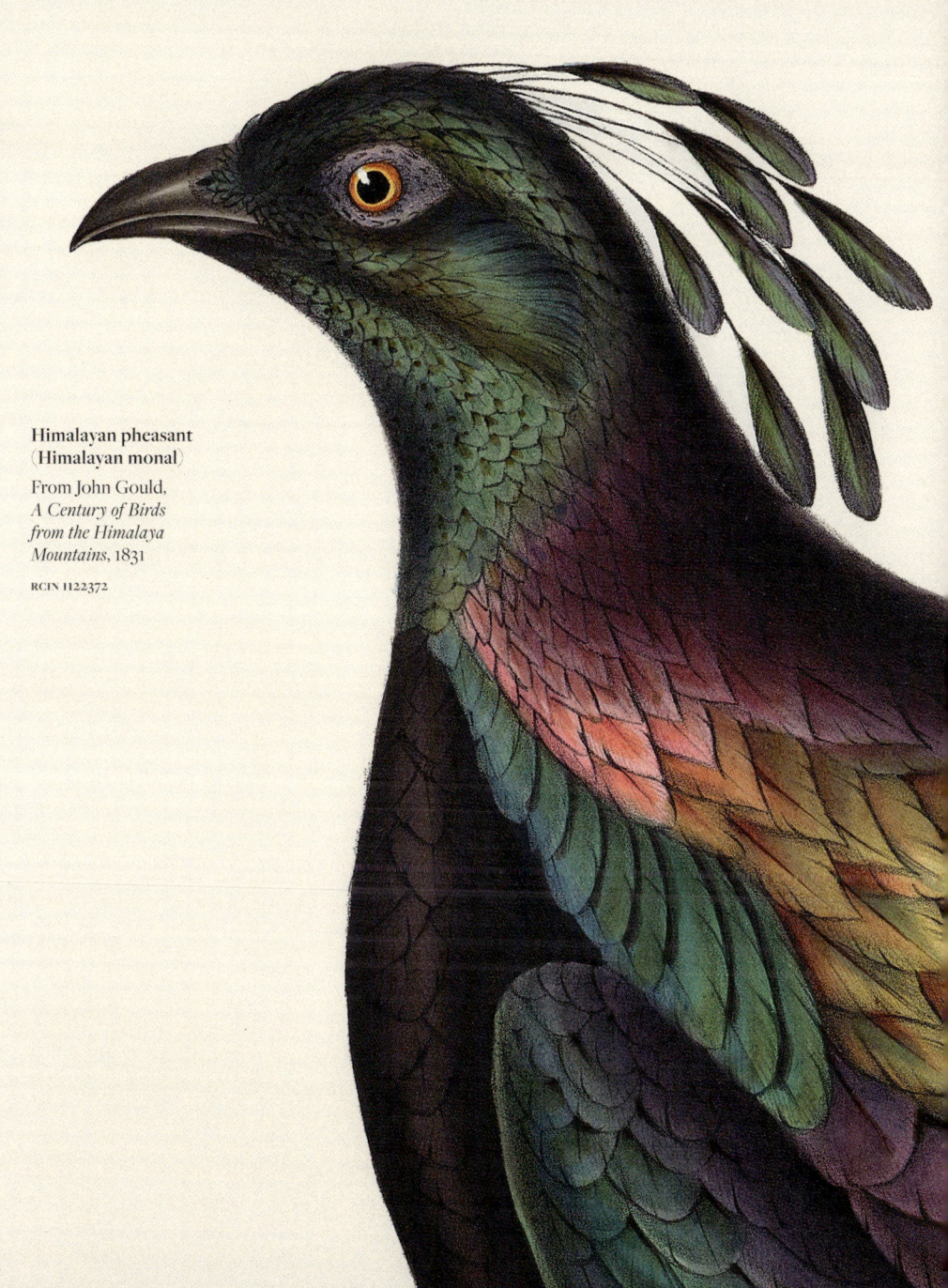

Himalayan pheasant
(Himalayan monal)

From John Gould,
A Century of Birds
from the Himalaya
Mountains, 1831

RCIN 1122372

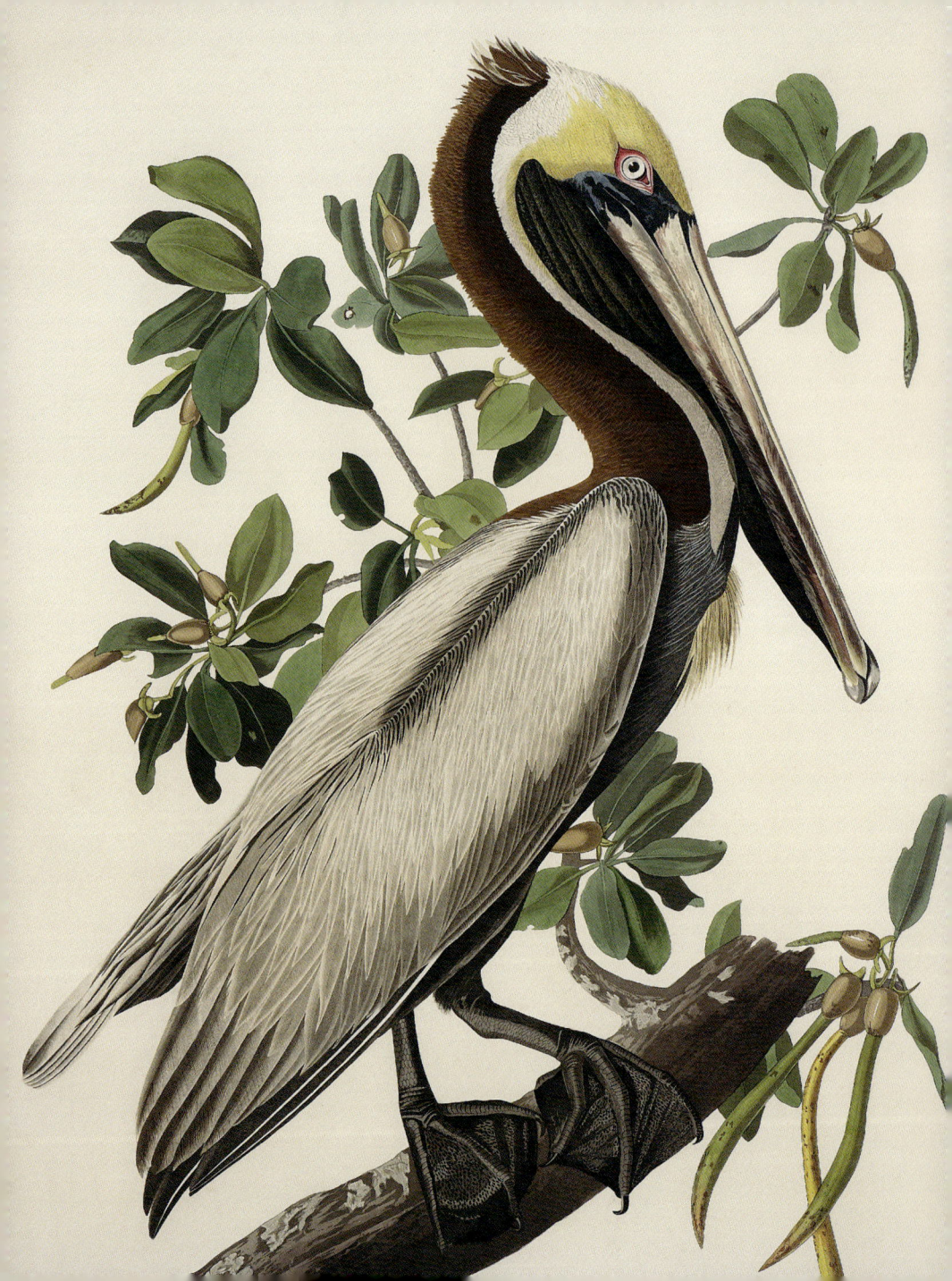

OPPOSITE

Brown pelican

From John James
Audubon, *The Birds
of America*, 1834–5

RCIN 1122504

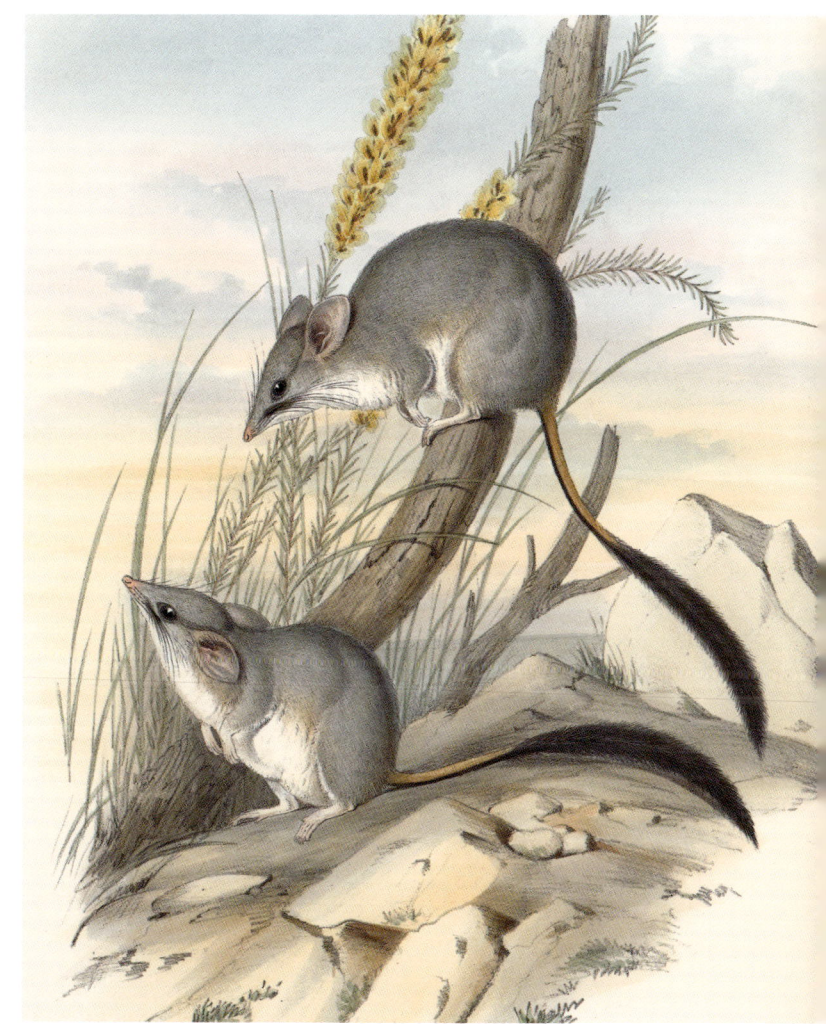

Handsome-tailed
phascogale

From John Gould,
*The Mammals of
Australia*, 1863

RCIN 1122359

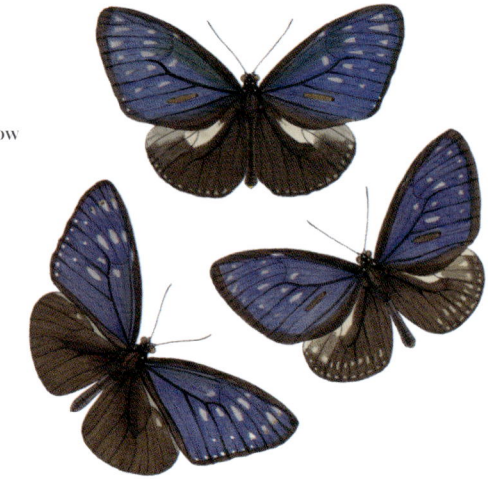

Assam blue-spotted crow

From Frederic Moore,
Lepidoptera Indica,
1890–2

RCIN 1089444

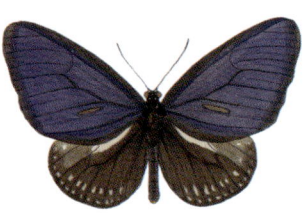

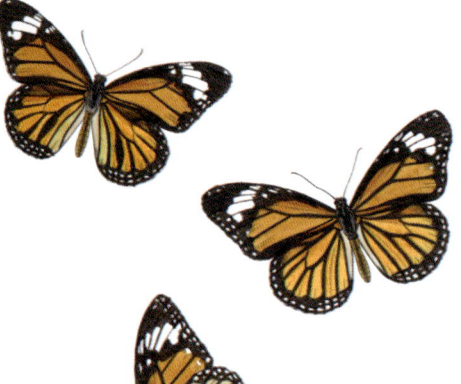

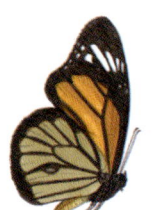

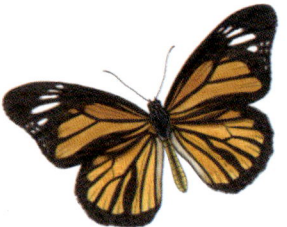

Common tiger

From Frederic
Moore, *Lepidoptera
Indica*, 1890–2

RCIN 1089444

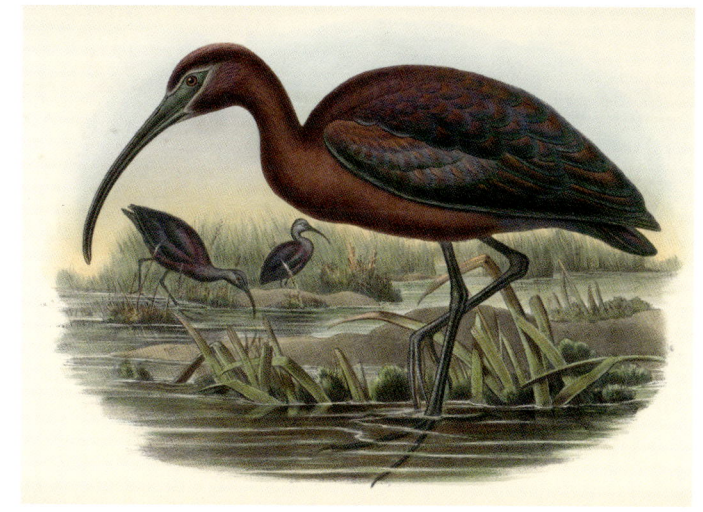

Glossy ibis

From John Gould,
*The Birds of Great
Britain*, 1873

RCIN 1122345

Scarab beetle

From Thomas
Martyn, *Paintings of
Natural History*, 1794

RCIN 1057112

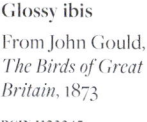

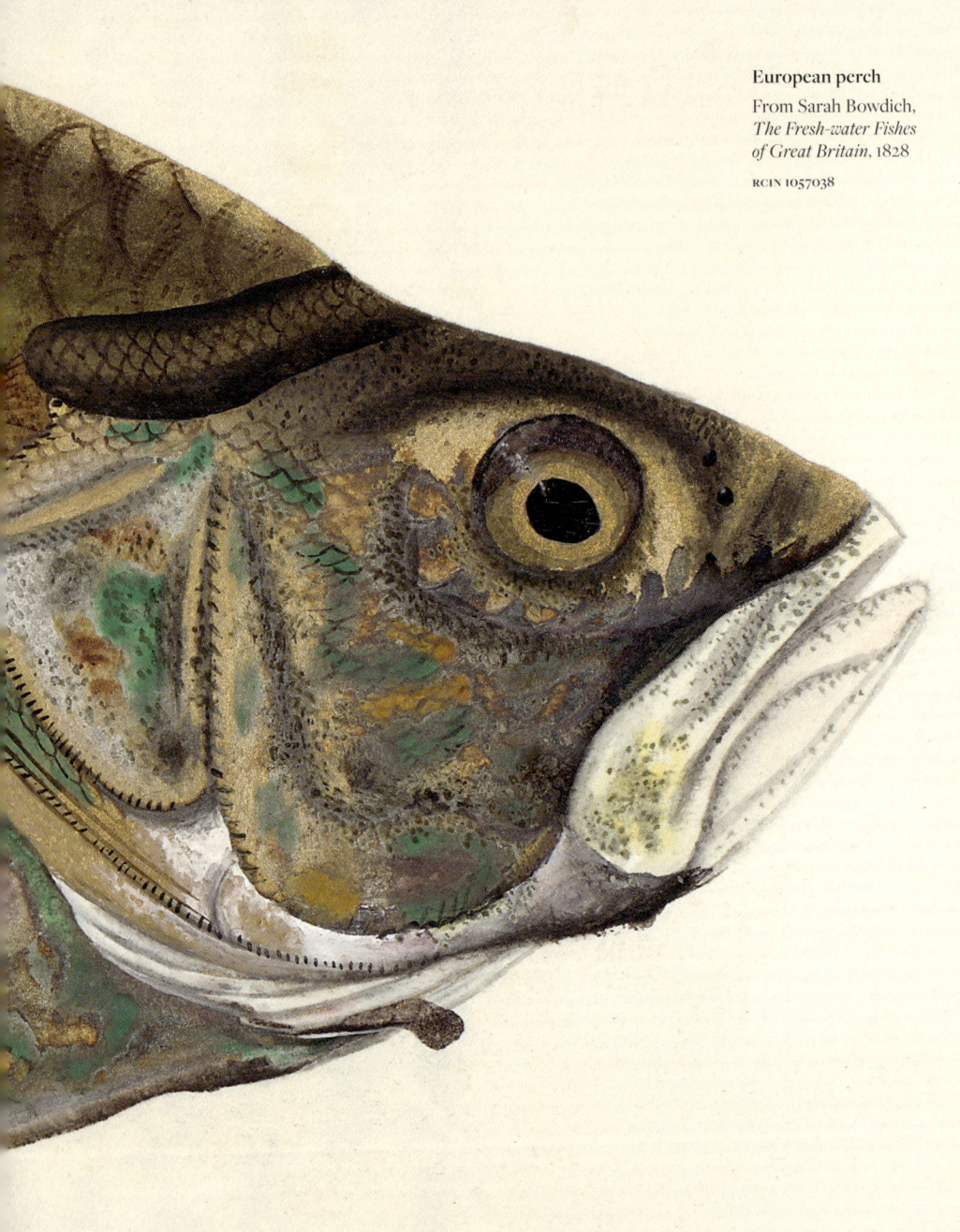

European perch

From Sarah Bowdich,
*The Fresh-water Fishes
of Great Britain*, 1828

RCIN 1057038

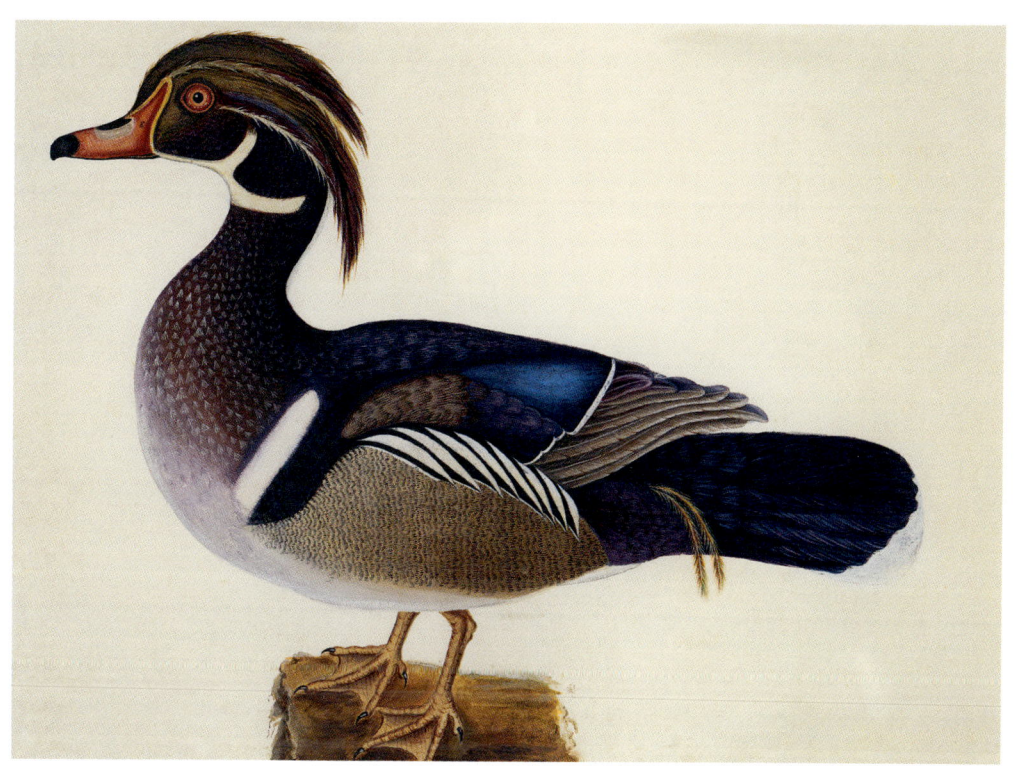

Summer duck

Mark Catesby,
c.1722–6

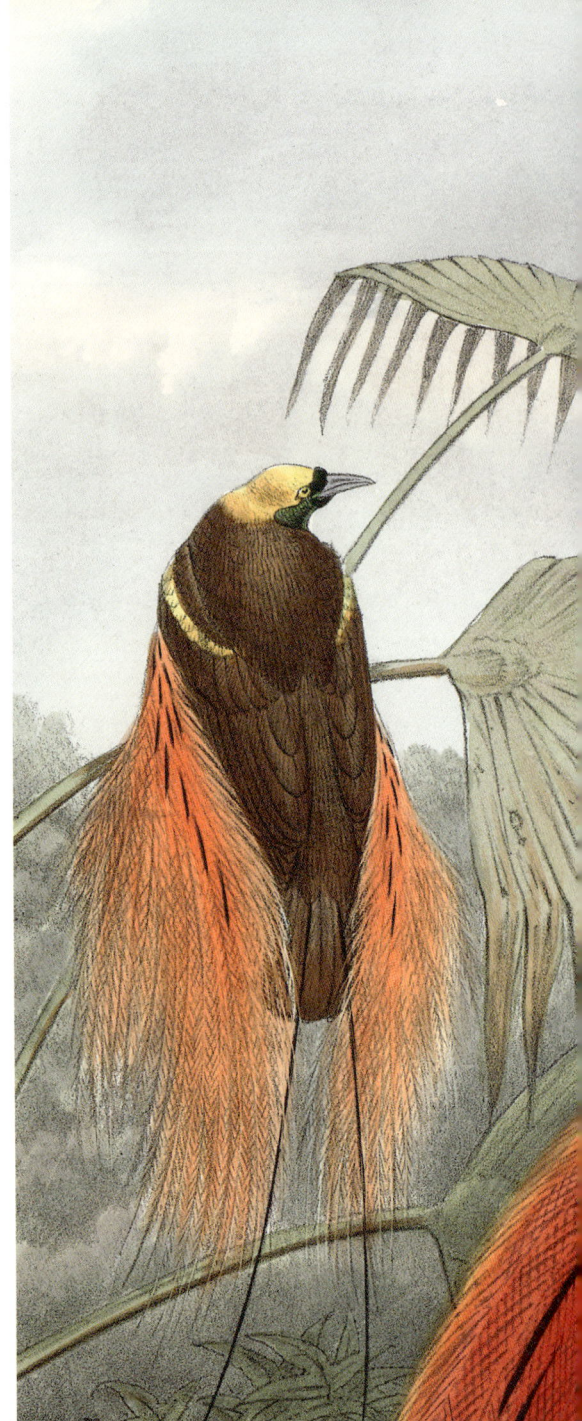

**Marquis de Raggi's
bird of paradise
(Raggiana bird of paradise)**

From John Gould, *The Birds
of New Guinea and the adjacent
Papuan Islands*, 1875–88

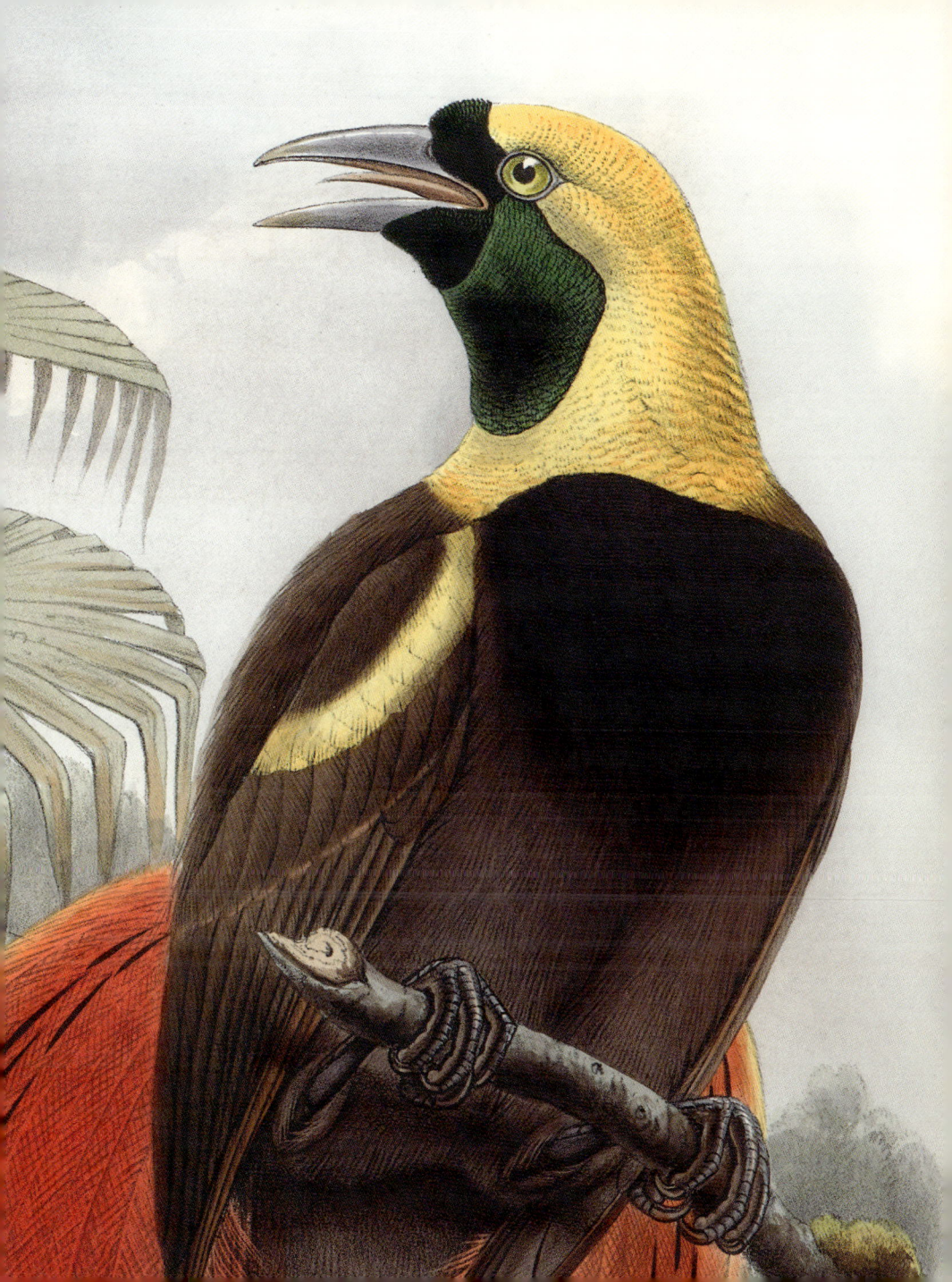

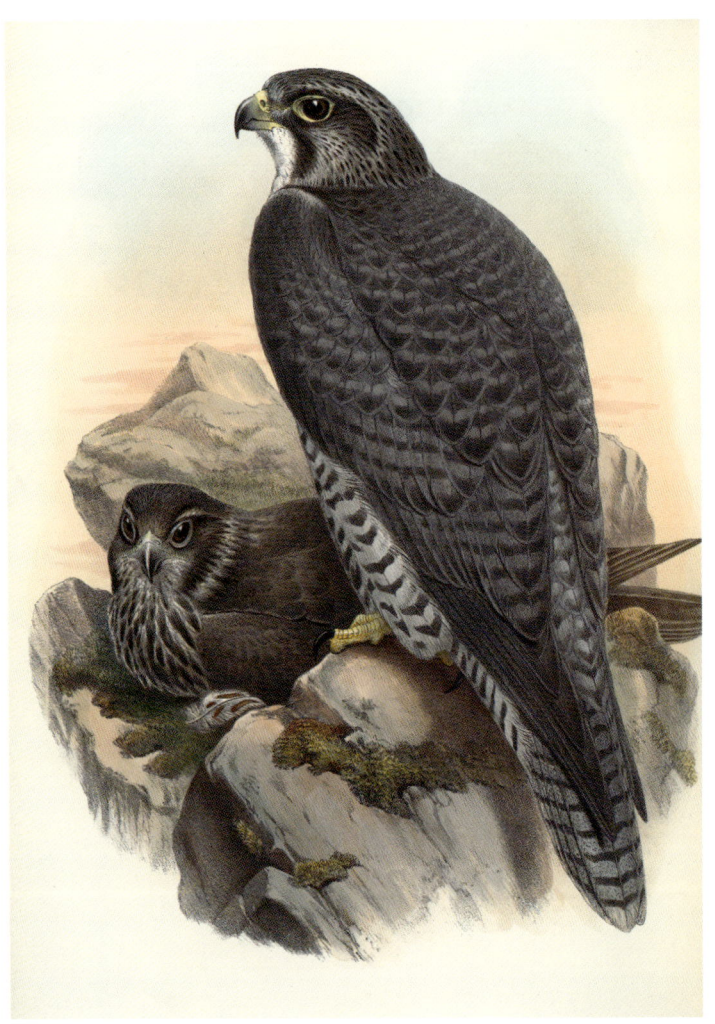

Norwegian falcon
(gyrfalcon)

From John Gould,
*The Birds of Great
Britain*, 1873

RCIN 1122342

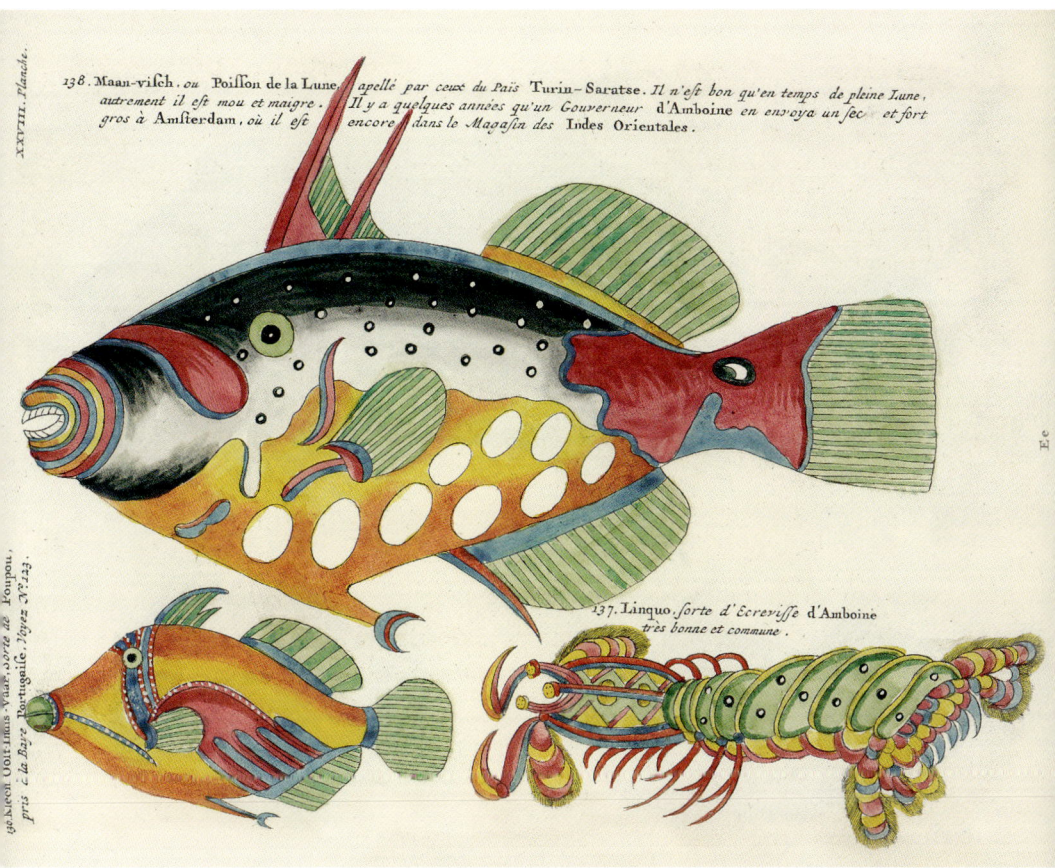

138. Maan-visch, ou Poisson de la Lune, apellé par ceux du Pais Turin-Saratse. Il n'est bon qu'en temps de pleine Lune, autrement il est mou et maigre. Il y a quelques années qu'un Gouverneur d'Amboine en envoya un sec et fort gros à Amsterdam, où il est encore dans le Magasin des Indes Orientales.

137. Linquo, sorte d'Ecrevisse d'Amboine très bonne et commune.

Fish and crustaceans

From Louis Renard,
*Poissons, Ecrevisses et
Crabes*, 1754

RCIN 1057042

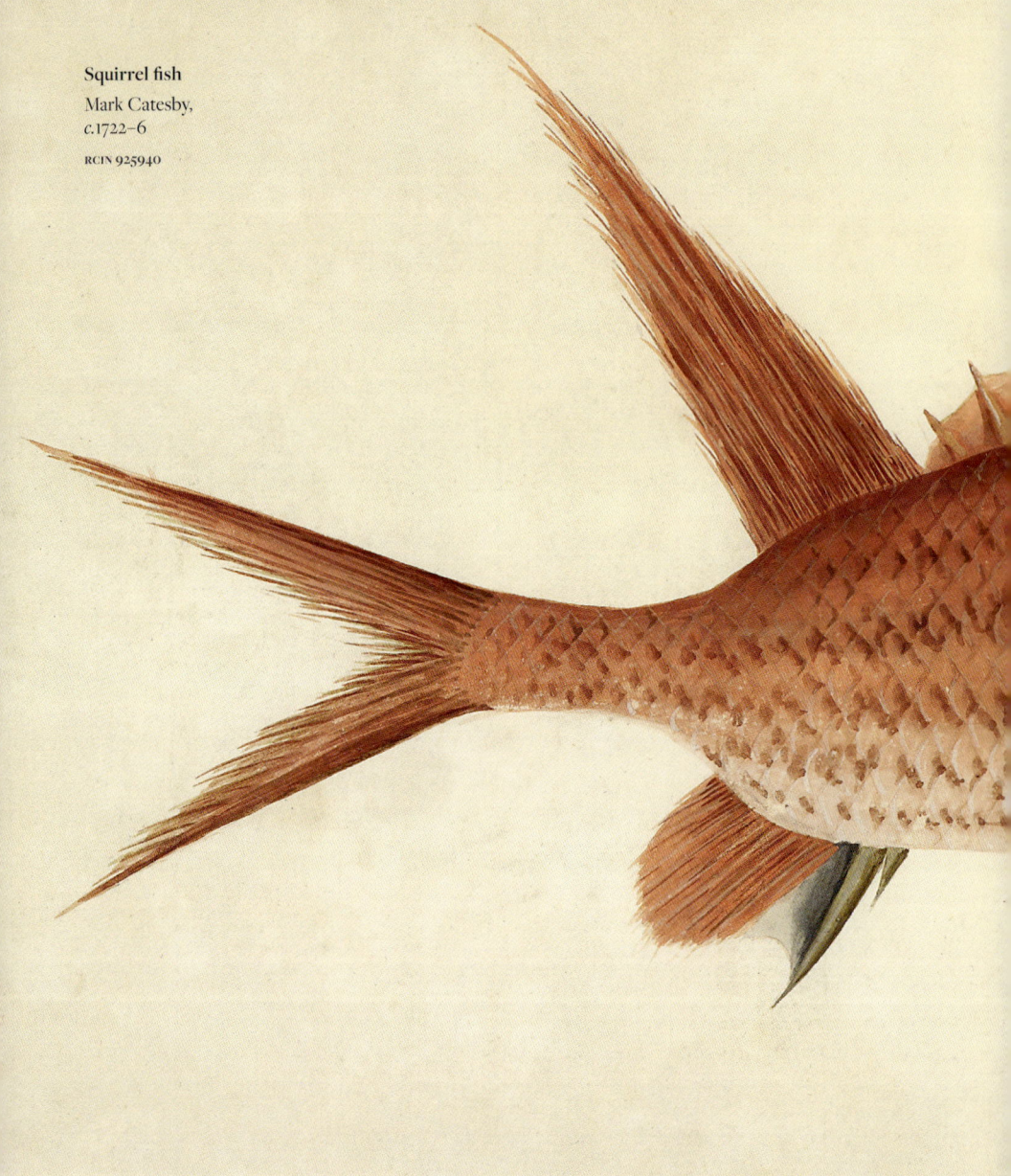

Squirrel fish

Mark Catesby,
*c.*1722–6

RCIN 925940

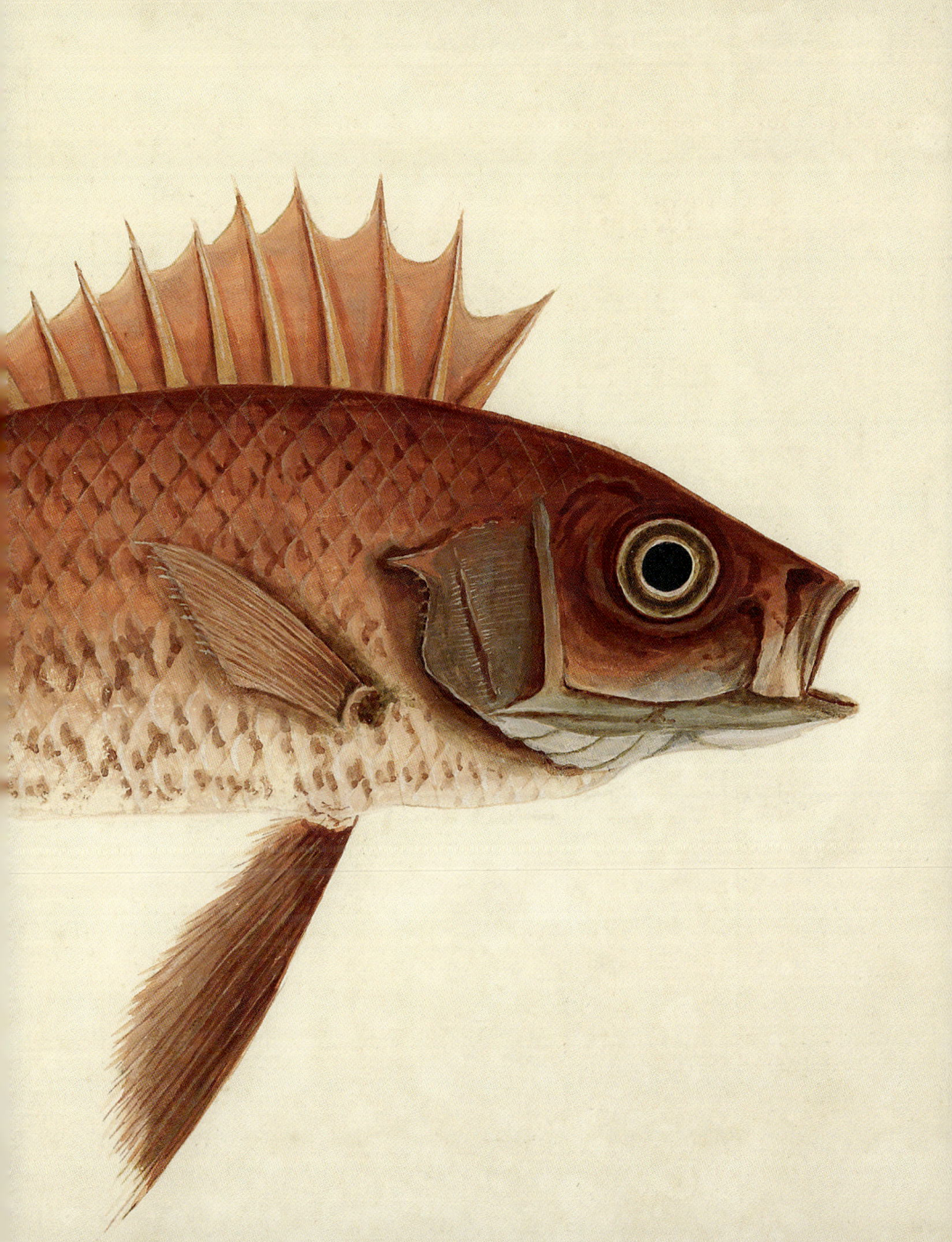

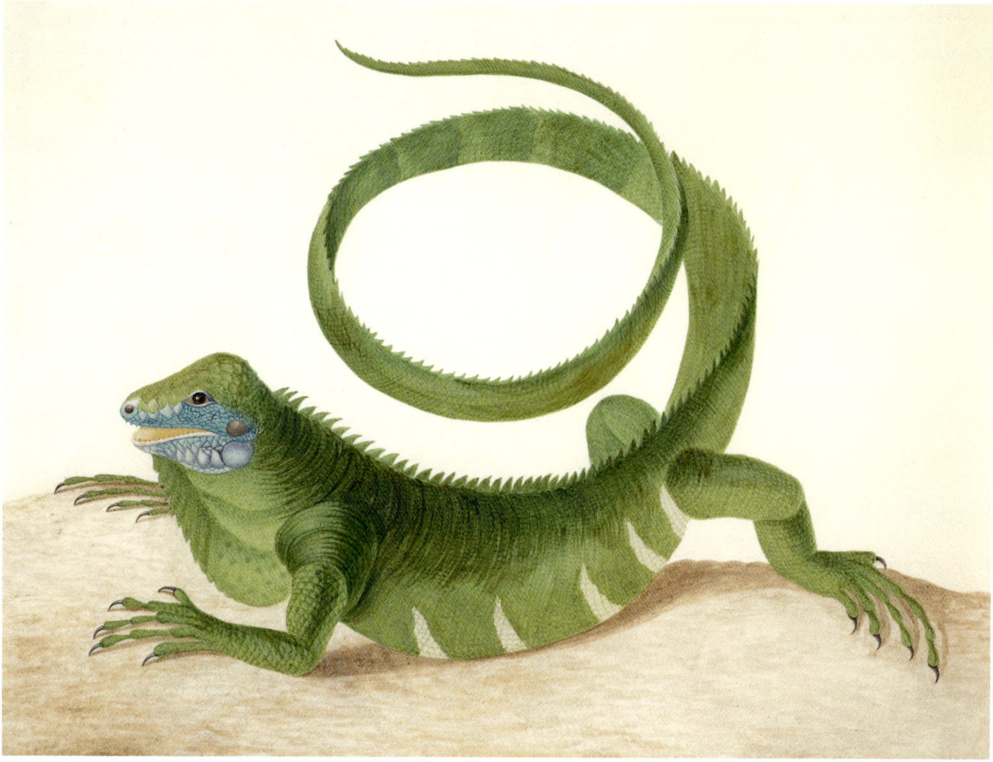

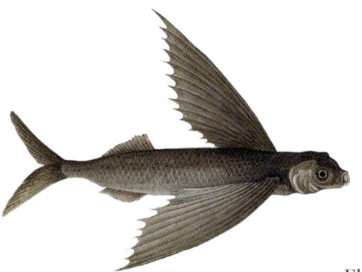

Green iguana

Workshop of Maria
Sibylla Merian, *c.*1705

Flying fish

Mark Catesby,
*c.*1722–6

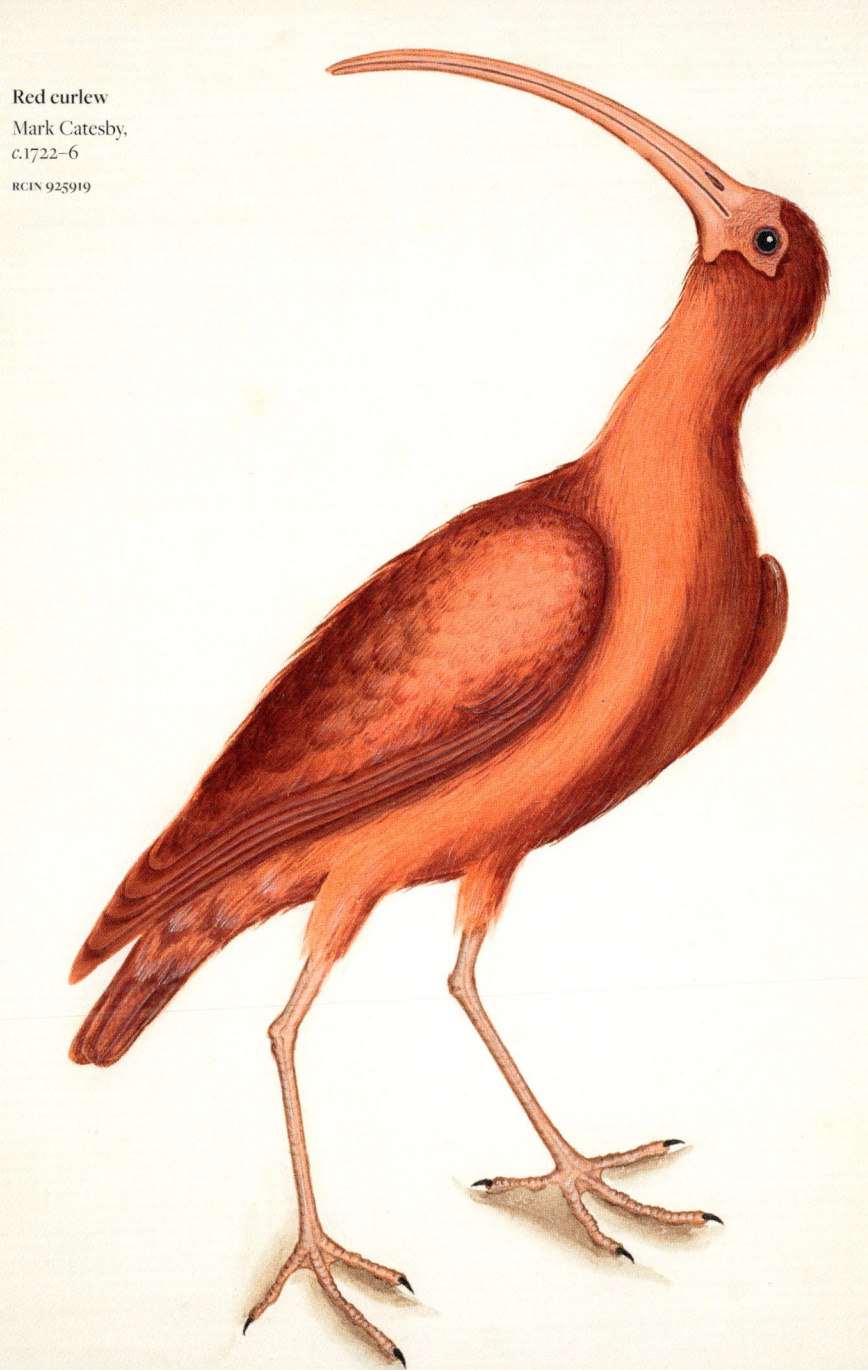

Red curlew

Mark Catesby,
*c.*1722–6

RCIN 925919

Further Reading

David Attenborough *et al.*, *Amazing Rare Things: the art of natural history in the age of discovery*, 2007

Daniela Bleichmar, *Visual Voyages: images of Latin American nature from Columbus to Darwin*, 2017

David Elliston Allen, *Books and Naturalists*, The New Naturalist 112, 2010

Jonathan Elphick, *Birds: The Art of Ornithology*, 2017

Kate Heard, *Maria Merian's Butterflies*, 2016

Robert Huxley (ed.), *The Great Naturalists*, 2007

Philip Kennedy, *The Bird: the great age of Avian illustration*, 2021

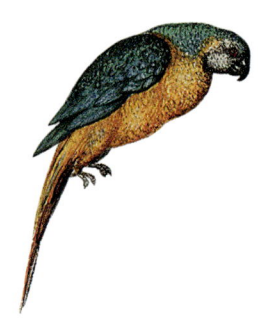

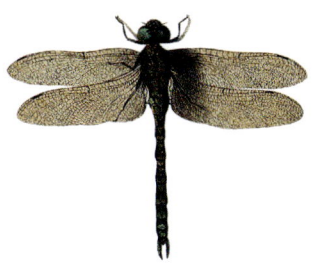

Henrietta McBurney, *Illuminating Natural History: the art and science of Mark Catesby*, 2021

Theodore W. Pietsch (ed.), *Fishes, Crayfishes and Crabs: Louis Renard's 'Natural History of the Rarest Curiosities of the Seas of the Indies'*, 1995

Malini Roy *et al.*, *Animals: art, science & sound*, 2023

Elisabeth Rücker and William T. Stearn, *Maria Sibylla Merian in Surinam: ... commentary to the facsimile edition of Metamorphosis*, 1982

Published 2025 by Royal Collection Trust
York House, St James's Palace
London SW1A 1BQ

© Royal Collection Enterprises Limited 2025 |
Royal Collection Trust

Introduction by Andrew Brown, Assistant Curator of
Books and Manuscripts, Royal Collection Trust

ISBN 978-1-909741-92-8

104665
10 9 8 7 6 5 4 3 2 1

A catalogue record of this book is available from the
British Library.

Designer: Matthew Wilson | www.mexington.co.uk
Concept design: Jevon Hall
Publisher: Kate Owen
Commissioning Editor: Anjali Bulley
Managing Editor: Polly Fellows
Production Manager: Sarah Tucker
Reproduction: DL Imaging
Printed on GallerieArt Matt 150gsm
Printed and bound in Slovenia by DZS Grafik

Royal Collection Trust publications
are distributed in North America by
The University of Chicago Press,
1427 East 60th Street, Chicago,
IL 60637 USA (press.uchicago.edu),
and throughout the rest of the world
by **Thames & Hudson Ltd.,**
6–24 Britannia Street, London
WC1X 9JD (thamesandhudson.com).

EU Authorised Representative:
Interart S.A.R.L.
19 rue Charles Auray,
93500 Pantin, Paris, France

productsafety@thameshudson.co.uk
interart.fr

Long-tailed tits

From John Gould,
*The Birds of Great
Britain*, 1873

RCIN 1122343

FRONTISPIECE

**Carolina parrot
(Carolina parakeet)**

From John James
Audubon, *The Birds
of America*, 1827–30

RCIN 1122502

TITLE PAGE

Bullfrog

Mark Catesby,
1722–6

RCIN 926025

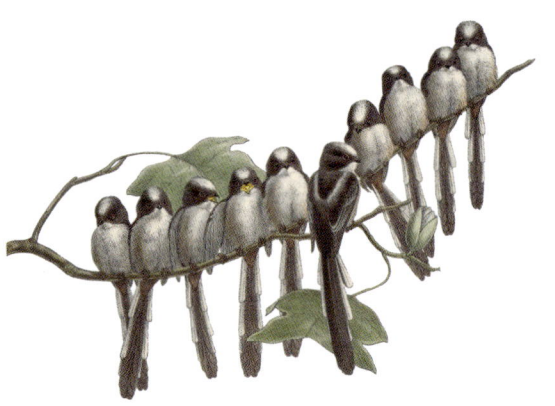